Busybody

A Comedy

Jack Popplewell

D1432023

Samuel French — London
New York - Toronto - Hollywood

JUL 1 6 2012

© 1965 BY JACK POPPLEWELL

Rights of Performance by Amateurs are controlled by Samuel French Ltd, 52 Fitzroy Street, London W1P 6JR, and they, or their authorized agents, issue licences to amateurs on payment of a fee. **It is an infringement of the Copyright to give any performance or public reading of the play before the fee has been paid and the licence issued.**

The Royalty Fee indicated below is subject to contract and subject to variation at the sole discretion of Samuel French Ltd.

Basic fee for each and every
performance by amateurs   Code M
in the British Isles

The Professional Rights in this play are controlled by Eric Glass Ltd, 28 Berkeley Square, London W1

The publication of this play does not imply that it is necessarily available for performance by amateurs or professionals, either in the British Isles or Overseas. Amateurs and professionals considering a production are strongly advised in their own interests to apply to the appropriate agents for consent before starting rehearsals or booking a theatre or hall.

ISBN 0 573 01515 5

Please see page iv for further copyright information

Printed and bound in Great Britain

BUSYBODY

Presented by Michael Codron, Audrey Lupton and Arthur Lane at the Duke of York's Theatre, London, on the 9th December 1964, with the following cast of characters:

(in the order of their appearance)

MRS PIPER	*Irene Handl*
RICHARD MARSHALL	*Andrew Laurence*
DETECTIVE CONSTABLE GODDARD	*Robin Lloyd*
DETECTIVE SUPERINTENDENT BAXTER	*Robert Cawdron*
CLAIRE MARSHALL	*Beryl Baxter*
MARIAN SELBY	*Ann Rye*
ROBERT WESTERBY	*Rodney Diak*
VICKIE REYNOLDS	*Frances Barlow*

Directed by HUGH GOLDIE

SYNOPSIS OF SCENES

The action of the play takes place in Richard Marshall's private office high up in a block of offices in London

ACT I

SCENE 1 Night
SCENE 2 Fifteen minutes later
SCENE 3 The following morning

ACT II

Six o'clock the following evening

ACT III

Four-thirty the following afternoon

COPYRIGHT INFORMATION

(See also page ii)

This play is fully protected under the Copyright Laws of the British Commonwealth of Nations, the United States of America and all countries of the Berne and Universal Copyright Conventions.

All rights including Stage, Motion Picture, Radio, Television, Public Reading, and Translation into Foreign Languages, are strictly reserved.

No part of this publication may lawfully be reproduced in ANY form or by any means—photocopying, typescript, recording (including video-recording), manuscript, electronic, mechanical, or otherwise—or be transmitted or stored in a retrieval system, without prior permission.

Licences for amateur performances are issued subject to the understanding that it shall be made clear in all advertising matter that the audience will witness an amateur performance; that the names of the authors of the plays shall be included on all programmes; and that the integrity of the authors' work will be preserved.

The Royalty Fee is subject to contract and subject to variation at the sole discretion of Samuel French Ltd.

In Theatres or Halls seating Six Hundred or more the fee will be subject to negotiation.

In Territories Overseas the fee quoted above may not apply. A fee will be quoted on application to our local authorized agent, or if there is no such agent, on application to Samuel French Ltd, London.

VIDEO RECORDING OF AMATEUR PRODUCTIONS

Please note that the copyright laws governing the video-recording are extremely complex and that it should not be assumed that any play may be video-recorded for whatever purpose without first obtaining the permission of the appropriate agents. The fact that a play is published by Samuel French Ltd does not indicate that video rights are available or that Samuel French Ltd controls such rights.

ACT I

SCENE 1

SCENE—*Richard Marshall's private office high up in a block of offices in London. Night.*

The room is attractively furnished, as befits the managing director of a flourishing development company. The main door is up C, leading to an ante-room and to the outer door. Another door down R leads to an inner office, and there is a fire door L. L of the main door is a small cupboard with the door opening on stage. A large bay window is angled across the up L corner of the room.

When the CURTAIN rises only the light over the table R is on. The L half of the room is in darkness. The window curtains are open, but the blinds are down. The main and outer doors are open.

MRS PIPER enters up C. She is very nervous. She goes to the telephone on the table R and dials a number, standing L of it. A draught shuts the door up C with a bang, and almost startles her into dropping the receiver.

MRS PIPER. Is that nine-nine-nine? . . . Good evening. I should like to report a murder, please . . . I thought that would make you jump—it did me . . . Yes. My name's Mrs Piper. I live at Chatham House, near Victoria Station . . . Where am I now? (*Irritably*) Well, I'm at Chatham House, near Victoria Station. I live in the basement. Only I'm not there now—I'm 'ere at the top floor, in the boss's office. 'E's Marshall Developments Limited . . . Oh, I don't know who the corpse is. (*She points*) He's there—along the passage—in Mr Logan's office. I only seen 'im when I went in to tidy up. I'm on the executive staff, you see. I'm the cleaner . . . Am I sure he isn't just having a nap? Well, he might be, but he's got about six inches of dagger in his back . . . You want me to—(*she repeats after him*) lock all the doors . . . Don't touch nothing . . . Keep me trap shut and wait till you arrive. 'Ere, hang on a moment, I'd better write this down. (*She puts the receiver down and goes to the main light switch up* C) Let's 'ave a bit of light on the subject. (*She switches on the lights, moves to the* R *end of the desk and picks up a pencil. She moves back to* C, *stops, and sees the body of a man over the chair* C. *A knife is "protruding" from his back. She moves quickly back to the phone, putting the pencil on the table*) Hello! The corpse from Mr Logan's office—he's in here now. And it's Mr Marshall! It's the boss! (*She replaces the receiver and exits hurried up* C *as the* LIGHTS *fade to Black-Out*)

CURTAIN

SCENE—*The same. Fifteen minutes later.*

When the CURTAIN *rises everything is exactly as at the close of the previous scene, except that the body is no longer there. The door up* C *is unlocked by* MRS PIPER *and opened by her. She moves aside and stands* L *in the doorway.* DETECTIVE CONSTABLE GODDARD *enters.*

MRS PIPER. 'Ere you are, dear. It's all yours. Well, if you'll excuse me, I'll bunk off now . . .

GODDARD. Hadn't you better show me where it is first? (*He looks around*)

MRS PIPER. Over there . . . (*She points over her shoulder to down* L)

GODDARD (*crossing to below the desk*) Here?

MRS PIPER. That's right. You can find me in the basement if you want me.

GODDARD. Just a minute. Are you pulling my leg? I don't see any dead body.

MRS PIPER (*turning*) You want your eyes tested, my dear boy. (*She goes to him*) He's plain enough to see, for goodness' sake. (*She points*) There!

(*They both stare at the empty chair*)

Oh, blige me! Well, it was there!

GODDARD. If this is a practical joke, I hope the Superintendent is amused.

(GODDARD *moves round to below the cupboard.* MRS PIPER *crosses above the desk to* L *of it*)

MRS PIPER. I'm telling the truth.

GODDARD. He's on his way here. Your report dragged him out of a warm bed.

MRS PIPER. I tell you, 'e was there. I saw 'im distinctly. (*She moves below the desk*)

GODDARD. Perhaps he's hiding somewhere?

(MRS PIPER *reacts.* GODDARD *laughs*)

In this cupboard perhaps. (*He opens the cupboard and a coat falls out. He picks it up, hangs it up and closes the cupboard*)

MRS PIPER. Now, don't be silly, dear. That's not funny.

GODDARD. All right, then, start at the beginning. In your own words. (*He moves to* L *of the armchair, taking out pen and notepad*)

MRS PIPER (*moving to* L *of Goddard*) First of all I saw it in Mr Logan's office. I ran straight down to tell my hubby. "Fred," I said, "Mr Marshall's been murdered." Fred can make quick decisions when an emergency arises. "Go back up there", he said, quick as a flash, "and telephone the police."

GODDARD. A man of action . . .

MRS PIPER. Yes.

(GODDARD *sits on the* L *arm of the armchair*)

So I did, only I didn't go to the office where the corpse was. I come in 'ere, and dialled nine-nine-nine. (*Crossing above the armchair to* R *of it*) And while they was taking down my particulars, I nearly 'ad a fit. 'E was draped over that chair.

GODDARD. A dead man?

MRS PIPER. Yes. It was the boss.

GODDARD. So where is he?

MRS PIPER. I dunno. I only know 'e was 'ere at the time. I don't know where 'e's took 'isself off to.

GODDARD (*rising to up* C) Superintendent Baxter won't like this little lot, madam.

MRS PIPER (*stepping down stage*) Crumbs. To hear you talk, anybody'd think I'd mislaid him. (*She moves below the armchair to* R *of Goddard*) 'Ere, what's he like?

GODDARD. The Super? A holy terror. He went home early to spend a couple of days in bed. (*He puts the pad and pen back in his pocket*)

MRS PIPER. Sounds like my old man. Once he goes to bed he usually stays flopped out for a couple of days.

GODDARD. I wouldn't like to be you if you've called him out on a false alarm. He's got a severe chill. (*He laughs*) I can't wait to see his face.

(MRS PIPER *moves towards the door*)

Where are you going?

MRS PIPER. I can't wait either.

GODDARD (*moving to* L *of Mrs Piper and turning her round*) I'm afraid you'll have to, madam. You've reported a murder.

MRS PIPER (*moving downstage*) And it's the last time I do, then.

(GODDARD *closes the door*)

It's more nuisance than it's worth. (*She looks about her, behind a chair, under a sheaf of papers*) I mean, how could a body disappear?

GODDARD. Especially when it was locked in. You did lock the door, I suppose?

MRS PIPER. 'Course I did. You saw me unlock it.

GODDARD. Perhaps he went thataway. (*He points to the door* R)

MRS PIPER. That door's locked permanent. (*Crossing above the armchair to* R *of Goddard*) Oh, there's one thing I didn't tell you. When I saw the body'd followed me in 'ere, I got out quick to tell Fred. "Fred," I said, "that body's got a crush on me . . ."

GODDARD. Mrs Piper, when did you lock the door?

MRS PIPER. Ten minutes later when I'd plucked up courage.

(GODDARD *turns away*)

Well, I don't care, I was shaken. The Superintendent is going to be shaken, too, isn't he? (*She sits in the armchair*)

GODDARD (*crossing to* R *of her*) He isn't noted for his sense of humour. They say if ever he smiled his face would crack. I suppose you hadn't been drinking?

MRS PIPER. No, I 'adn't! Leastways, not enough to make me see double.

(*The outer door slams and footsteps sound in the ante-room, followed by a loud nose-blow*)

GODDARD. Sounds like the chief.

MRS PIPER (*crossing down* L *of the desk*) Sounds like the whole bloomin' tribe.

(GODDARD *opens the door up* C. SUPERINTENDENT BAXTER *enters briskly*)

GODDARD (*cheerfully*) Good evening, sir. (*He closes the door and moves to* R *of the armchair*)

BAXTER (*moving down* C; *very curtly*) Ugh! (*He blows his nose*) Would happen to me, wouldn't it? I'd have given six months of my pension to stay in bed. (*He blows his nose loudly*) Well, where is it?

GODDARD. The body, sir?

BAXTER. Yes, the body.

GODDARD. Well, as a matter of fact, we don't know, sir.

(BAXTER *suspends "operations" on his nose*)

BAXTER. *What* did you say?

GODDARD. It appears to have gone, sir.

BAXTER (*in a voice of doom*) It's—*what?*

GODDARD. Gone, sir. (*He steps back*) This is the lady who reported the murder. Mrs Piper, sir.

(MRS PIPER *moves toward Baxter via below quite happily, with no further signs of nervousness. She is greeting an old friend*)

MRS PIPER. 'Arry Baxter!

(*They stare at her.* MRS PIPER *moves in to* L *of Baxter*)

Well, strike a light if it isn't you.

GODDARD (*shocked*) This, madam, is Detective Superintendent Baxter.

MRS PIPER. Not to me it ain't. (*To Baxter*) Well, be all that's wonderful, 'aven't you got on! I love your hat.

(BAXTER *takes off his hat.* MRS PIPER *crosses below him to* L *of Goddard*)

We used to live down the same street in Ealing. He married my second cousin. I told her, I said "he'll be as good as two hot-water bottles in a cold snap". (*Turning to Baxter*) 'Ere, don't you say you've forgotten who I am. Lily Piper. Lily 'Arper as was.

BAXTER. Yes—well—(*putting his hat on the chair down* L *and remaining* LC) we'll talk about that later.

MRS PIPER (*crossing to* C) When 'e said the Superintendent was a holy terror I was petrified.

(GODDARD *steps in*)

(*To Goddard*) I thought you said 'e'd no sense of humour. Scared stiff I was. And look what came in! You. (*She faces Baxter*)

BAXTER. If something is amusing you, Goddard, I have sufficient sense of humour to wish to share the joke.

GODDARD. No, sir.

(MRS PIPER *moves to* R *of Baxter*)

MRS PIPER. "If ever he smiles", he says, "his face will crack," he says.

(GODDARD *turns and moves to up stage of the armchair*)

It's nice to see your old friends getting on in their perfession.

BAXTER (*crossing below Mrs Piper to* L *of the armchair*) I am waiting for your report, Goddard.

GODDARD (*moving down stage*) Well, sir, under the circumstances…

MRS PIPER (*moving* R) He ain't got nothing to report, darling. There was a dead body in here, but when I brung this gentleman in, it was gone. And don't you say I'm suffering from delucinations, 'cos I don't 'ave 'em.

GODDARD. No signs of a body, sir.

BAXTER. You reported the dead man was your employer, Richard Marshall.

MRS PIPER. In Mr Logan's office he was. (*She points*)

BAXTER. You understand it's a very serious offence to summon the police without justification?

MRS PIPER. I tell you he was on that chair.

BAXTER. You said he was in Mr Logan's office.

MRS PIPER. He was in here, too.

BAXTER. Where?

MRS PIPER (*moves down* L *of the chair*) On this chair. (*She strikes it*)

BAXTER (*crossing to up* R *of the chair*) Well, it isn't here now. (*He strikes the chair*)

MRS PIPER. Well, it was.

BAXTER. Well, where is it?

MRS PIPER. 'Ow should I know! It must have trotted off somewhere. (*She moves down* L)

GODDARD (*crossing above the armchair to* R *of Baxter*) Mrs Piper was instructed to lock the door, sir. Unfortunately a period of ten minutes elapsed between her going out and obeying instructions.

BAXTER (*turning* L) They told you to lock the door so that nobody could interfere with the room.

MRS PIPER. Yes, well, so I did do when I'd calmed down.

BAXTER. You should have done it straight away.

MRS PIPER. It's all right you being wise after the horse has flown. (*She sits on the chair down* L, *then rises holding Baxter's hat*) Harry—I've crumpled your hat. (*She hands the hat to Baxter then returns to her seat*)

(BAXTER *turns away to face front, holding the hat out in his hand*)

GODDARD (R *of Baxter*) What do you think, sir?

BAXTER. Without resorting to blasphemy, Goddard, I am unable to reply to that question.

GODDARD. Yes, sir.

(BAXTER *suddenly sneezes and crosses down* R)

MRS PIPER. Bless you!

BAXTER (*blows his nose fiercely*) I should be in bed with a hot-water bottle!

GODDARD. Yes, sir.

(MRS PIPER *rises and crosses below to* L *of Baxter who is punching out his hat*)

MRS PIPER. 'Ere, there was a wonderful cure on the telly last night. You get an onion, Harry, are you listening? Don't peel it, and bung it in your ear . . . (*She suddenly breaks off*) 'Ere, look at my hand. That's you, getting me all excited . . .

(GODDARD *moves to* L *of Mrs Piper*)

I must 'ave banged the woodwork when I hit that chair.

GODDARD. There's blood on your hand, too, sir.

BAXTER. Ugh? (*He looks at his hand*)

GODDARD. The chair, sir.

(GODDARD *moves to* R *of the chair, via above the armchair.* BAXTER *moves to* L *of the chair via below the armchair, and Mrs Piper.* MRS PIPER *moves up to* R *of Goddard*)

BAXTER. It *is* blood.

MRS PIPER. Serves you right, getting peevish. (*Suddenly*) 'Ere, do you mean it's from the . . . ? I've been and licked it now. I think I'm going to faint.

(BAXTER *puts his hat on the desk.* GODDARD *goes to her*)

But it's all right. I never do. Now, perhaps you'll be sorry you called me a liar, 'Arry Baxter.

BAXTER (*indicating the door down* R) Where's that lead to?

MRS PIPER. That's Mr Westerby's office.

(BAXTER *crosses Mrs Piper to the door down* R)

The door's locked permanent. (*She follows to the door, pulling on Baxter's coat*) You 'ave to enter it along the passage . . .

(BAXTER *opens the door and goes out. He turns on the light.* GODDARD *steps down* C)

Well, I never saw it open before.

(BAXTER *comes back to* R *of Mrs Piper*)

Is anyone there, 'Arry?

BAXTER. No, anyone isn't there, 'Arry. Give me the key to Logan's office. You did lock *that*, I hope.

MRS PIPER. 'Course I did. I did as I was told.

BAXTER. All right! May I have the key?

MRS PIPER. I haven't got it.

BAXTER. Where is it?

MRS PIPER. In the keyhole.

BAXTER (*sighing*) In the keyhole! Thank you very much. (*To Goddard*) Take a look, Goddard. You never know. (*He takes off his coat*)

(GODDARD *exits up* C *and to* R)

MRS PIPER (*following him*) First door on the right down the passage. Next to the la-la.

(BAXTER *puts his coat on the chair up* R)

When you walked in you could have knocked me down with a feather.

BAXTER. Really? (*Moving to* L *of the armchair and turning it to face* R) Madam.

MRS PIPER (R *of the armchair*) Oh, I'm a madam now, am I? Gone up in the world, have we? Reached 'eady 'eights. Forgotten our old friends.

BAXTER. I certainly haven't forgotten you.

MRS PIPER. No, I should think not. The times you nipped into our kitchen for a quick drag when you were supposed to be trying shop door-handles . . .

BAXTER. Things have changed since then!

MRS PIPER. Your feet haven't.

BAXTER (*loudly*) Sit down! (*Quietly*) Please!

MRS PIPER. Thank you.

(*They sit:* MRS PIPER *in the armchair,* BAXTER *below the table* R)

BAXTER. Now then, tell me your story from the beginning.

MRS PIPER. You mean, after you left Benson Street?

BAXTER (*yelling*) No! (*Quietly*) You have discovered a dead body. I would like to hear the details.

MRS PIPER. Oh! In my own words?

BAXTER (*nods*) As few as possible.

MRS PIPER. Well . . .

BAXTER. Briefly, please. I'm a busy man. (*He looks at his watch*)

MRS PIPER. If you interrupt before I start it's going to take a long time, isn't it? I can't recollect my thoughts, can I? (*Expansively*) We-ell, now, let me see . . .

BAXTER. You are employed as an office cleaner by Mr Richard Marshall.

(MRS PIPER *purses her lips, folds her arms and hums*)

Go on!

MRS PIPER (*with ironic apology*) I beg your pardon. I was under the impression *you* was telling *me*.

BAXTER (*with a sigh*) In your own words.

MRS PIPER. I *was* employed by Mr Richard Marshall as an office cleaner. My hubby also was employed—as the caretaker. You remember Fred? He won't half be pleased when I tell him I've seen you. He's in bed. Sprained his back reading the *Sunday Times*. A week ago Mr Marshall gave him the sack.

BAXTER. Did he indeed! Why?

MRS PIPER. He said he was too careless to be a caretaker. He said he got so wrapped up in what he was doing he forgot to stoke the boilers.

BAXTER. What was he doing?

MRS PIPER. Drinking. Leave off! (*She laughs*) He's a chap can only do one thing at a time.

BAXTER. So he got the sack . . .

MRS PIPER. Oh, yes, but that's nothing wonderful. Mr Marshall had a nasty habit of going round sacking people. Made himself very unpopular, I can tell you. One thing you'll find plenty of, 'Arry, is people who aren't sorry he's departed.

BAXTER. Are you one of them?

MRS PIPER. I'm sorry about the way he went, but I can't say I'm sorry he's gone.

(GODDARD *enters up* C)

GODDARD. No sign of a body, sir.

BAXTER (*rising*) Any sign of forcible entry?

GODDARD. None, sir.

BAXTER. You'd better check in here.

GODDARD. Right, sir. (*He closes the door, crosses* L *to check the fire exit, then slowly moves round the windows checking the blinds, then moves down stage of the desk chair*)

BAXTER. How many keys are there to these offices? How many people could let themselves in and out?

MRS PIPER. Well, there was Mr Marshall, and Mr Marshall's private secretary, Miss Selby, and me acting on behalf of Fred. Oh, and there's a fourth key Mr Marshall kept locked up inside his desk.

BAXTER (*moving to below the cupboard*) Show me.

MRS PIPER. I can't. Nobody can't open Mr Marshall's desk. It's private.

BAXTER. I'll bet you can.

MRS PIPER (*pulling out a bunch of keys*) Well, there might just happen to be one on my bunch that . . .

BAXTER. Open it.

MRS PIPER (*rising and crossing below Baxter to above the upstage end of the desk*) Please! Proper little Lord Fauntleroy you turned out to be. (*She unlocks a drawer*) It'll be at the back, dear, behind the partition.

(BAXTER *looks in, standing* R *of her,* GODDARD L)

BAXTER. Where? I can't see it.

MRS PIPER. Oh, no more can I. It's gone. (*She closes and locks the drawer*)

BAXTER (*moving up* C) So it has. (*To Mrs Piper*) So Mr Marshall dispensed with your husband's services?

(MRS PIPER *follows to* L *of Baxter.* GODDARD *moves round the desk chair to the* R *end of the desk*)

MRS PIPER. That's right. You remember Fred? He'll be tickled pink when he knows I've made your acquaintance after all these years. It must be—twenty years. I bet you've got quite a family now! I say—(*meaningfully*) we didn't have to wait long for the first one, did we? (*She crosses below Baxter and sits in the armchair*)

BAXTER (*very hastily*) Goddard—wait outside!

GODDARD (*smiling*) Yes, sir. (*He crosses above Baxter to the door up* C)

BAXTER. And Goddard . . .

GODDARD. Sir?

BAXTER. Look in the toilet.

GODDARD. What for, sir?

BAXTER (*angrily*) Anything you might find! (*He moves down* LC)

GODDARD. Yes, sir.

(GODDARD *exits up* C, *closing the door*)

MRS PIPER. Isn't he cultured? They probably wouldn't have had you today, 'Arry.

BAXTER. Mrs Piper! Because, many years ago, we were acquaintances, I am endeavouring to be very patient with you. But . . .

MRS PIPER. We were more than acquaintances. You took me out once. (*Coyly*) I'll bet you've arrested people for less than what you tried to . . .

(BAXTER *crosses above to* R *of her*)

BAXTER. Shall we carry on?

MRS PIPER (*reminiscently*) Proper ball of fire you were, twenty years ago. Now where was I? Oh, yes, about Mr Marshall's corpse . . . Where had I got to?

BAXTER. You didn't get anywhere! (*He takes out a notepad and a pen*)

MRS PIPER. Like you when you took me out!

BAXTER. I have an idea. I will ask the questions—and you answer them. It will save a lot of time. (*He sits below the table* R)

MRS PIPER. That's a very good idea.

BAXTER. First of all—this is Richard Marshall's private office. Is that correct?

MRS PIPER. It was when he was alive. The whole ruddy block belongs to him. 'E was Marshall's Developments Ltd.

BAXTER. Adjoining is Mr Westerby's office?

MRS PIPER. That's right. 'E's the accountant. 'E's only young, but 'e's a marvellous 'ead for figures. He shins up the columns like a . . .

BAXTER. Mr Logan is across the passage?

MRS PIPER. Not now he isn't, dear. He's away on holiday in the South of France. He's the brains of the outfit. Very clever. Got his B.O. at Oxford.

(BAXTER *reacts*)

My hubby always says he wouldn't trust him farther than he can throw the piano.

BAXTER. You mean he's dishonest.

MRS PIPER. No, of course I don't. I just mean he's all there with his dolly drops. But he's ever such a nice fella. Do you know what he . . .

BAXTER. Please confine your answers to yes or no. Now who else is employed here?

MRS PIPER. Yes.

BAXTER (*turning his chair to face the desk, and flinging his notebook down*) All right, in your own words.

MRS PIPER. Well. (*She rises and stands* L *of Baxter*) There's Mr Marshall's secretary, Miss Selby. Proper potty about the boss she is.

BAXTER. Do you mean she's in love with him?

MRS PIPER. Well, I suppose you could put it like that.

BAXTER. How do you know?

MRS PIPER. I know everything that goes on around here.

BAXTER. I'll bet you do.

MRS PIPER. I don't half get some laughs out of emptying the waste-paper baskets. Miss Selby was thirty-four last February. But she looks thirty-five. I'd give her thirty-five easy. Then there's young Vickie. She's the typist. Victoria Reynolds. Nice little kid . . . She'll be twenty next August. (*She moves above the armchair*)

BAXTER. Is she in love with Mr Marshall?

MRS PIPER. No fear. She's gone on Mr Westerby. I don't blame her neither. He's tall and sunburned with a split chin and smashing eyes. Like pickled walnuts and he speaks beautiful—like a railway announcer. He'll be thirty-two in July. Got a beauty spot on his right shoulder.

BAXTER. And who is *he* in love with?

MRS PIPER. Me. (*She taps herself*) Leave off! I wish he was. No.

I've always been faithful to Fred. Ruddy fool. I ought to have my head examined.

BAXTER. Mr Marshall—your employer—is he married?

MRS PIPER (*returning to* L *of the table*) Oh, yes. He'll be leaving the most beautiful widow. Her name's Claire. Very chick! Beautiful hands with long, hand-painted finger-nails. I like her. She always speaks to me when I see her—if she don't see me first.

BAXTER. And Logan? Who is he?

MRS PIPER. I beg your pardon, dear?

BAXTER. Logan, who is he?

MRS PIPER. He's the planner. But he's on holiday, so it couldn't be him. I mean, he couldn't have murdered Mr Marshall when he wasn't here, could he?

BAXTER. Might he have killed him if he *had* been here?

MRS PIPER. Oh! Yes. I expect so.

BAXTER. What I mean is, had they quarrelled?

MRS PIPER. Oh, yes. He hated him!

BAXTER. Oh, did he, indeed! (*He rises, crosses below to* C *and puts his pen and pad away*)

MRS PIPER. But don't get steamed up about that. Everybody hated him. He never thought of people as people. Expendable office equipment—that's all we was to him.

BAXTER. Did you hate him?

MRS PIPER. No, I didn't 'ate 'im. I just couldn't stand the sight of 'im.

(BAXTER *moves to the downstage end of the desk.* MRS PIPER *follows to* R *of him*)

'Ere, *I* didn't do it, if that's what you're hinting at.

BAXTER. Somebody did—according to you. (*He picks up a double photograph from the desk*) Is this Mrs Marshall?

MRS PIPER. That's right.

BAXTER. Who's this?

MRS PIPER. That's *Mr* Marshall.

BAXTER (*surprised*) This is Marshall? I've met him.

MRS PIPER (*at a tangent*) Then that makes six of us.

BAXTER. Six what?

MRS PIPER. Suspects. Except I didn't do it.

BAXTER. Are you suggesting *I* did?

MRS PIPER. Anybody who knew Mr Marshall could have murdured him. Including you.

BAXTER. I am here, madam, as an investigator. (*Loudly*) Not as suspect number one! (*He replaces the photo and calls*) Goddard!

MRS PIPER. I saw a play on the telly where the detective turned out to be the murderer. Went mad with a meat axe. Power lust.

(GODDARD *enters up* C, *closing the door*)

BAXTER. Power lust! (*Moving to* L *of Goddard*) Find anything?

GODDARD. No, sir.

BAXTER. What time is it now? (*He examines his watch*) Five-past midnight. (*To Mrs Piper*) Why were you going the rounds of the building so late at night?

MRS PIPER. I told you—my hubby's the caretaker. Only he's in bed with a split disc.

BAXTER. Was the outer office door locked?

MRS PIPER. Of course it was.

BAXTER. Hm. Better get Marshall's home on the phone.

GODDARD. Right, sir. (*He crosses above Baxter to above the desk*) You don't happen to know the number do you, madam?

MRS PIPER. Yes, dear. (*Follows to up* C) It's Mayfair o-one-two-four.

GODDARD (*dialling*) Thank you so much.

MRS PIPER. Pleasure.

BAXTER. Better make sure he isn't in bed snoring where I ought to be. (*He puts his left hand in his pocket*)

MRS PIPER. Well, if he is he'll be ruddy uncomfortable with that dagger sticking out of his back. Whee! (*She plunges her right hand through his arm*)

GODDARD (*on the telephone*) Oh, Mrs Marshall—sorry to disturb you. C.I.D. here—Z Division, Detective Superintendent Baxter would like to speak to you, please.

MRS PIPER (*to Baxter*) Hasn't he got beautiful manners? (*She passes Baxter below her to the phone*) Go on, dear, don't be shy.

BAXTER (*taking the receiver*) Hello, Mrs Marshall? Could I speak to your husband, please? . . . He's not at home?

MRS PIPER (*digging him with her elbow*) There you are!

BAXTER (*changing the receiver to his left hand*) I'm so sorry, Mrs Marshall, I missed that. No, it's just a routine inquiry. If he does return will you let me know? The number is . . .

MRS PIPER. Victoria one-three-one-three.

BAXTER. Victoria one-three-one-three .

(MRS PIPER *moves up* C)

Thank you. (*He hangs up*) She says he often stays out all night.

GODDARD. What do you think, sir?

BAXTER. Well, on the strength of her evidence I suppose we'll have to investigate. Get Willis on the blower.

(GODDARD *dials.* BAXTER *crosses to* L *of Mrs Piper*)

You seem to have started something.

MRS PIPER. I ain't started nothing.

BAXTER. What time does the staff get here in the morning?

MRS PIPER. Nine o'clock, more or less. Vickie's always last. Miss Selby's always first. Comes very prompt, she does, with flowers to put on the boss's desk. She's the only one who'll miss him.

GODDARD. Your call, sir.

(BAXTER *takes the receiver and sits at the desk.* GODDARD *steps round* R *of him to stand up* R)

BAXTER (*on the telephone*) Willis? Baxter . . . I've been called out on a possible murder case. That's it—Chatham House. I'm not sure because—hold on to something, Willis!—the corpse has disappeared. That's it—you heard me all right . . . I don't know . . . I'm not sure the witness is very reliable.

MRS PIPER (R *of Goddard*) Well, I like that!

BAXTER. Oh, she's honest enough. As a matter of fact she's known to me . . . No, no, she hasn't a police record—(*looking at Mrs Piper*)

(MRS PIPER *reacts*)

I knew her when I was on the beat.

MRS PIPER. I'll say.

BAXTER. Under the circumstances we've got to assume she's speaking the truth. There's a chair here. I'd like it examined for bloodstains. I shall also need the fingerprint boys here. And circulate a description of Richard Marshall. There's a photograph of him here. According to the witness he's been murdered. Let's have some action right away. (*He replaces the receiver*)

(MRS PIPER *moves to the upstage end of the desk and leans on Baxter's hat. She hands it to him. He puts it on the downstage end of the desk*)

MRS PIPER (*admiringly*) Weren't you *masterful!*

(GODDARD *moves to* R *of her*)

'Ere, what did the bloke say about me having a police record? Cheek! (*To Goddard*) The only time I had trouble with the police was when I walked out with him.

BAXTER (*hastily*) Goddard!

GODDARD (*quickly; moving up* C) Sir?

BAXTER. Take a look outside.

(GODDARD *moves up to* L *of the door up* C. BAXTER *rises, moves round the downstage end of the desk and crosses up* R *for his coat*)

Wait a minute. I'll come with you. We shall have to wait until our chaps get here. Then we shall have to be here first thing when the staff arrive. (*He sneezes*)

MRS PIPER. Bless you!

BAXTER (*putting on his coat*) A glass of whisky would do me a world of good.

(GODDARD *opens the door and stands* L *of it*)

B

Mrs Piper (*moving to* L *of Baxter*) What you need is a jolly good rubbing in back and front with that new linctus they keep advertising. It's got V-fifteen in it, the secret ingredient. I know what's best for you.

Baxter. You know a lot, you do. (*Crossing below her into the doorway*) Oh, by the way—(*he turns, smiling ironically*) when you find out who did the murder, you will let me know, won't you?

Mrs Piper. Yes, I will. But it isn't going to be easy, is it, if you keep losing all the bodies.

Baxter *exits up* C. Mrs Piper *follows him, and* Goddard *goes last, closing the door, as—*

the Curtain *falls*

SCENE 3

Scene—*The same. Eight-forty-five, the following morning.*

The bloodstained chair C *has been removed, the armchair reset, and the blinds opened.*

When the Curtain *rises* Baxter *is standing down* L, *blowing his nose.* Mrs Piper *enters up* C, *carrying a waste-paper basket.*

Mrs Piper. Ain't it no better, 'Arry? (*She puts the basket under the desk and moves to* R *of Baxter*)

Baxter. What do you think? Mrs Piper!

Mrs Piper. Yes, dear?

Baxter. There's something I want to make clear to you. As you are the only material witness I suppose you'll have to stay. But when I start asking these people questions, I want to hear what they have to say and not what you have to say.

Mrs Piper. Well, I know you do, 'Arry.

Baxter. And another thing, don't call me 'Arry.

Mrs Piper. It was 'Arry when I first knew you.

Baxter. Well, it isn't now!

Mrs Piper. What is it? 'Enry?

Baxter. When we're alone you can call me anything you like. In front of other people you will refer to me as Superintendent Baxter. If you please! (*He crosses up* R, *takes the chair from up* R *and puts it* C, *below the upstage end of the desk*)

Mrs Piper. All right. I'll try and remember. (*She moves away* LC)

Baxter. Thank you.

Mrs Piper. I keep forgetting how important you are. It's a good thing you're there to remind me. I say, I *was* proper proud when you were on the telephone to Mrs Marshall. Putting all the aitches in and all that . . . I bet she thought she was talking to a gentle-man.

BAXTER. Mrs Piper . . .

MRS PIPER. No, 'Arry, no! That's very hurtful. You can call me what you like in front of the others but when we're alone my name is Lily.

(BAXTER *turns*)

No, 'Arry, say it. Lily.

BAXTER. Certainly not. (*He tries to move away but she stops him*)

MRS PIPER. Lily.

BAXTER. Lily.

MRS PIPER. That's better. (*She moves down* L *and sits*)

(GODDARD *enters up* C)

GODDARD. Mrs Marshall has arrived, sir. (*He steps to* R *in the door-way*)

(CLAIRE MARSHALL *enters up* C. *She is an attractive woman in her thirties. She is genuinely distraught*)

BAXTER. Come in, Mrs Marshall. I'm Superintendent Baxter.

(GODDARD *exits, closing the door*)

CLAIRE. This is appalling. I simply don't understand. Your assistant just told me that my husband has been killed.

BAXTER. Yes, it would appear so, madam. I'm sorry.

CLAIRE (*crossing below him to down* L) He says you found him, Mrs Piper.

MRS PIPER. That's right, dear.

CLAIRE. How awful. Oh! (*She turns away*)

BAXTER. Will you sit down? (*He points to the chair* RC)

CLAIRE (*moving to the desk and putting her bag on it*) No, I'm all right. I mean, I shall be. (*She takes out her handkerchief and turns*) I'm afraid I can't help at all. Sometimes he stays out. It didn't occur to me to report him as missing. Our marriage was far from perfect.

BAXTER. You don't suspect anyone?

CLAIRE. No, I can't think of anybody who'd want to . . . want to . . . (*She seems to be about to faint*)

MRS PIPER (*rising*) Now sit down, dear. (*She leads her to the arm-chair*) We've got to ask a few questions, haven't we, to get to the bottom of it. (*Frowning at Baxter*) We shall try to be as tactful as we can. There! Now, when did you last see your husband?

(BAXTER *coughs loudly and points to the chair down* L. *She scurries back to her chair and sits down* L)

BAXTER. I will decide which questions to ask, Mrs Piper. (*To Claire*) Now, Mrs Marshall, when did you last see your husband?

MRS PIPER (*sotto voce*) 'S what I said!

CLAIRE. Yesterday morning when he left for the office. He had a business appointment for lunch. Later he phoned to say he wouldn't be home for dinner.

BAXTER. And you've no idea why anybody should wish to attack him?

CLAIRE. Well, he had an unfortunate manner. He could be quite ruthless. He made enemies.

BAXTER. Anyone in particular?

CLAIRE. No. It's just—he wasn't very kind to people who stood in his way.

MRS PIPER. Telling me!

(GODDARD *knocks on the door up* C *and enters*)

BAXTER (*moving up stage*) Hang on a minute!

(GODDARD *pushes the door to*)

BAXTER. It's my intention to see everybody in here. (*He crosses above the armchair and turns* R *of Claire*) Perhaps you'd prefer to wait in another room.

CLAIRE. I don't mind staying in here, Superintendent.

BAXTER (*moving down* R) No, I'd rather you did wait elsewhere. Wait in Mr Westerby's office. I'll call you if I need you.

CLAIRE. Oh, very well, if you insist. (*She rises and crosses down* R) Will you be keeping me here long?

BAXTER (*at the door down* R) That depends on the progress I make, Mrs Marshall.

CLAIRE. In that case I'd like to make one or two phone calls.

BAXTER (*opening the door*) Certainly.

CLAIRE. Thank you.

(CLAIRE *crosses him and exits down* R. BAXTER *closes the door*)

GODDARD. Anything so far, sir?

BAXTER. No, she hasn't noticed anything unusual.

MRS PIPER. I have. (*She rises*)

BAXTER. I am conducting the case, Mrs Piper, thank you.

MRS PIPER (*moving* C, *above the armchair*) I know you are. But you need all the help you can get. If I notice anything unusual, it's my duty to draw it to your attention.

BAXTER. Very well. Draw it!

MRS PIPER. 'Ere, you know when you asked me what she was like—Mrs Marshall, I mean—and I said pretty. With long painted finger-nails. Very smart. Well, she hasn't!

BAXTER. Hasn't what?

MRS PIPER. Got long finger-nails.

(BAXTER *fidgets*)

No, that's very funny, 'Arry, you know. Ever since I've known 'er, they was long, and today they was short.

BAXTER. And what, pray, is your deduction? (*He turns away*)
MRS PIPER. She's cut 'em.
BAXTER. Thank you for sharing with me the products of your observation, Mrs Piper. I might have come to the same conclusion. (*He crosses below her to* L. *To Goddard*) Show Miss Selby in.

(GODDARD *exits up* C, *leaving the door open*)

MRS PIPER (*moving above the armchair to* R *of the chair* C) I'd want to know why she's cut 'em.
BAXTER (L *of the chair* C) It is my intention to assemble the entire staff in this office. But I am prepared to make an exception in your case . . .
MRS PIPER. I was only doing my duty.
BAXTER. If you don't shut up . . . !

(MARIAN SELBY *enters up* C)

(*Seeing her; quietly*) Oh! Good morning, Miss Selby. (*He crosses below Mrs Piper to* L *of Miss Selby*)

(MRS PIPER *follows him to* L *of Baxter*)

MARIAN. This is horrible! Too horrible for words!

(GODDARD *goes out, closing the door*)

BAXTER. You are Mr Marshall's private secretary.
MARIAN. Yes.
MRS PIPER. I told you.
BAXTER. How long have you been with the firm?
MRS PIPER. Eight years.
BAXTER. Did you enjoy working for him?
MRS PIPER. Not 'alf.

(BAXTER *points down* L. MRS PIPER *moves* L *and sits as before*)

BAXTER. Please sit down, Miss Selby.

(MARIAN *sits in the armchair.* BAXTER *sits* C)

MARIAN. He was a wonderful man. I loved every moment of it. He was so clever, so charming, and so very thoughtful.
MRS PIPER (*to herself*) Oh, oblige me!
MARIAN. I can't believe he's . . . Is there no doubt?
BAXTER. Not according to Mrs Piper. When did you last see him?
MARIAN. Last evening. Half past seven. I stayed late because we were expecting a call from New York. There was some delay, so Mr Marshall said I could go.
BAXTER. Was he still here when you went home?
MARIAN. Yes, he was.
BAXTER. Was the outer office door locked when you left?
MARIAN. Of course. I shut it behind me.

BAXTER (*rising and moving* R *of the desk*) Miss Selby, as his secretary, you were close to him. Do you know of anyone who might have felt animosity towards him?

MARIAN. Lots of people. People who resented the power of his personality. He suffered fools impatiently. (*Looking at Mrs Piper*) He demanded the very best of everyone. Often their best wasn't good enough.

MRS PIPER. Have you anyone particular in mind?

BAXTER (*to Mrs Piper*) I'm warning you.

MARIAN. I don't think I ought to contribute towards the gossip.

BAXTER (*moving to* C) The circumstances are too serious to tread delicately, Miss Selby. According to Mrs Piper he has been murdered. Any help you can offer will be thoroughly justified.

MARIAN. I suppose that's true. All right—then I suggest you might speak to his wife.

BAXTER. I already have.

MARIAN. She wasn't in love with him, you know. There was someone else.

BAXTER. How do you know that?

MARIAN. As you remarked, I was very close to him.

MRS PIPER. Not as close as you'd like to have been.

BAXTER. Was he in love with her?

MARIAN. How could he be? He was very distressed about her. She was ruining his life.

BAXTER. Do you happen to know the name of the man—her lover?

MARIAN. Yes. (*She hesitates*)

BAXTER. Well?

MRS PIPER. Come on, dear. (*She rises and moves to* L *of Baxter*) Don't keep us in suspenders.

MARIAN. You understand this is not something I can prove. I know it to be true, but it isn't evidence I could swear to in court. Do you still want me to answer?

MRS PIPER. Yes, please.

MARIAN. It was Mr Westerby.

BAXTER. Oh?

MRS PIPER. Coo! You fib! (*She steps in below Baxter*)

BAXTER (*pulling her back, crossing above the armchair to* R *of Marian and indicating the door down* R) That's the man who occupies that office?

MARIAN. Yes.

BAXTER. You think he was having an affair with Mrs Marshall?

MARIAN. I know he was.

BAXTER. I see. You say many people disliked him. Who else had you in mind?

MARIAN (*indicating Mrs Piper*) I suppose she gave the impression that she approved of him?

MRS PIPER (L *of Marian*) Who, me?

Baxter. On the contrary, Mrs Piper admitted she didn't like him.

Marian. That was very disarming of her.

Mrs Piper. 'Ere, what are you getting at?

Baxter (*crossing below the armchair to between them*) I said I will ask the questions, thank you, Mrs Piper.

Mrs Piper. Well, *you* ask her what she's getting at.

Baxter (*to Marian*) What are you gettin' . . . ? (*He scowls, turns and points to the chair down* L)

(Mrs Piper *sits down* L)

Marian (*to Baxter*) Her good-for-nothing husband was under notice to leave.

Mrs Piper. Good-for-nothing?

Marian. They resented it. They'd have lost their flat.

Mrs Piper (*rising*) 'Arry, that's a libel.

Baxter (*crossing below Marian, pushing Mrs Piper down in her chair, and continuing to below the desk*) Will you sit down! (*He puts his hand on the desk, facing up stage*)

Mrs Piper. Aren't you strong! Well, she shouldn't have said it. Poor fella. The doctor said he's never seen a worse case of malingering.

Marian (*rising to* C) When Mr Marshall fired him, did he or did he not threaten him with violence?

Mrs Piper (*rising*) 'E certainly did not! What he said was: "Somebody ought to lie in wait for you in a dark alley and hit you on the head with a tree trunk." That's what 'e said, but 'e never threatened him. (*She crosses to down* R)

Marian (*to Baxter*) Need I say more?

Baxter (*moving in*) But you have no proof linking anybody with Mr Marshall's death?

Marian. No proof.

Mrs Piper. Thanks for those few nuts.

(Goddard *enters up* C)

Goddard. Robert Westerby is here, sir.

Baxter. One moment, Goddard.

(Goddard *shuts the door*)

One other question, Miss Selby. You have a key to these offices?

Marian. Yes. (*She takes her bag from the desk*)

Baxter. You have it with you?

(Marian *shows it*)

And it hasn't recently been out of your possession?

Marian. No. (*She replaces the key in her bag*)

Baxter. Thank you, Miss Selby.

(MARIAN *puts her bag on the desk and moves up to the cupboard*)

I'll see Westerby now. (*He moves* C)

(GODDARD *exits, closing the door*)

MRS PIPER. 'Arry. 'Arry!

(BAXTER *and* MARIAN *both turn to her*)

BAXTER. I beg your pardon.
MRS PIPER. Well, Sarge—or whatever you call yourself.
BAXTER (*moving to* L *of her*) What is it now?

(MARIAN *takes off her coat*)

MRS PIPER. If she says she left the office at half past seven Big Ben must have had the hiccoughs. (*To Marian*) It was striking quarter to eight when I saw you go.
MARIAN (*hanging her coat in the cupboard and closing it*) The Superintendent asked me when I last saw Mr Marshall. (*She picks up her bag and moves* LC) I replied truthfully, half past seven. It so happens I came back to pick up some papers. I didn't see him, but I heard him in the washroom.
MRS PIPER (*primly*) Oh, well. Just as long as we've got that point established. Carry on, Super!

(ROBERT WESTERBY *is shown in up* C. GODDARD *goes out.* WESTERBY *is good-looking, a nervous individual, highly strung.* BAXTER *indicates for Marian to sit down*)

BAXTER (R *of Westerby*) Robert Westerby?
WESTERBY. Yes.

(MARIAN *sits down* L. MRS PIPER *pushes* BAXTER'S *right hand out so he is forced to shake hands with Robert*)

MRS PIPER. This is my friend, Superintendent 'Arry Baxter.
ROBERT. How do you do?

(*They shake hands.* MRS PIPER *sits at the table down* R)

I say, this is a shock for everybody!
BAXTER. Not for everybody, Mr Westerby. Someone must have known about it.
ROBERT. None of us, I imagine.
BAXTER. Sit down, please.
ROBERT. Thank you. (*He moves down stage*)
BAXTER. How long were you employed by Mr Marshall?
ROBERT. Two very long years.
BAXTER. Did you like him?
ROBERT. Did anybody?
BAXTER. Answer the question, please. (*He sits on the* L *arm of the armchair*)

ROBERT (*sitting* c) No, I'm afraid I didn't. Everybody disliked him. Oh—with the possible exception of Miss Selby.

MARIAN. Why do you say, "With the *possible* exception"?

ROBERT. I sometimes wondered if even your emotions weren't a sort of love-hate complex. Whatever that may mean.

MARIAN. How can you *say* that?

ROBERT. Sorry, I suppose I find it difficult to believe that anyone could love him.

BAXTER. You disliked him very much?

ROBERT. Passionately, but I'm not strong enough in nerves to kill anybody. And, anyway, why should I? He paid me very well.

BAXTER. What time did you see him last?

ROBERT. Six o'clock, when I left the office.

(MRS PIPER *rises and taps Baxter on the shoulder*)

BAXTER. And then you went straight home?

ROBERT. Yes.

(MRS PIPER *taps Baxter on the shoulder again*)

BAXTER (*turning*) You are dying to say something, Mrs Piper? No!

MRS PIPER. All right, then, only I was under the impression you wanted everybody's corporation. I know Mr Westerby wouldn't kill nobody. He's too nice to . . .

BAXTER. No doubt, Mrs Piper, you will eventually receive an official invitation to assist me in the prosecution of this case. (*Loudly*) Until then . . .

MRS PIPER. That isn't all I was going to say.

BAXTER. I didn't suppose it was! (*He rises and moves to up stage of the desk*)

MRS PIPER (*moving to* R *of Robert*) Only you didn't leave the office at six o'clock. You're mistaken.

ROBERT. My goodness, you're right!

(BAXTER *turns*)

Sorry. I'd have remembered later. It was about half past six.

MRS PIPER. More like twenty to seven.

(BAXTER *moves in between them*)

BAXTER. Why were you so late?

ROBERT. I'd been out during the afternoon. It must have been about six o'clock when I got back. I'd a few things to attend to.

BAXTER (*to Mrs Piper*) Do you agree with that statement?

MRS PIPER. That's right. I was just popping over to the "Bunch of Grapes" to fetch a jug of draught beer—Fred fancied some for his tea—I 'adn't got farther than the corner, when I bumped into Mr Westerby.

ROBERT. Yes, that's correct.

(BAXTER *crosses above Robert to* L *of him.* MRS PIPER *sits on the* L *arm of the armchair*)

BAXTER. Mr Westerby, you came back here about six o'clock and remained for forty minutes. Was Mr Marshall still here when you left?

ROBERT. The light was still on in his office.

BAXTER. You didn't see him?

ROBERT. No.

BAXTER (*to Marian*) Miss Selby, you left at seven-thirty and came back again to collect some papers. You left at—seven-forty-five. You say you heard Mr Marshall in the washroom, but you didn't see him either. Are you quite sure of that?

MARIAN. Naturally I didn't see him. But I've every reason to believe he was here.

BAXTER. Why?

MARIAN. I told you he was expecting a call from New York. Besides he had a business appointment at eight-fifteen. He said it was very important.

BAXTER. Who with?

MARIAN. A Mr Warfield.

BAXTER. Who is he?

MARIAN. I'd never heard of him before.

MRS PIPER. No more have I . . .

BAXTER. Even so, you can't swear that he was here?

(MARIAN *shrugs. She is convinced that her statement is irrefutable.* BAXTER *turns* R)

MRS PIPER. I suppose she heard the—you know! (*She mimes the toilet chain*)

MARIAN (*coldly*) I heard water iss-suing from the tap.

MRS PIPER. Oh!

BAXTER. It could have been someone else?

MARIAN. I suppose so.

(BAXTER *paces thoughtfully above the armchair*)

MRS PIPER. If it had been someone else she wouldn't have heard water iss-suing.

(BAXTER *moves to* R *of the armchair*)

I mean, the murderer wouldn't stay for a wash-and-brush-up, would he?

BAXTER. Why not? (*He turns back above Mrs Piper*)

MRS PIPER. Why, what do you mean . . . ?

BAXTER (*in a grisly voice,* R *of Mrs Piper, in her ear*) Blood.

MRS PIPER (*rising,* L *of Baxter*) Oh, no. 'Arry, don't.

BAXTER (*to Mrs Piper*) So you are the only person who was in the building most of the time.

MRS PIPER. I told you. I was out getting Fred's refreshment.

BAXTER. How long would that take? Ten minutes?

MRS PIPER. Oh, no, a bit longer. I had a couple myself while I was there.

BAXTER. Then how long were you?

MRS PIPER. I know exactly when I got back. It was ten past eight by the clock our daughter gave us for our silver wedding.

BAXTER. Ten past *eight?*

MRS PIPER. Which means it was ten past seven. Fred never got around to altering it after we put the clock back. So we de-duct one hour.

BAXTER. I see. (*He moves away to* RC)

MRS PIPER (*turning to Robert*) Until they put it forward again and then we're right for another six months. (*She moves up stage to the desk chair and sits*)

BAXTER (*to Robert*) Mr Westerby, you say you disliked Mr Marshall. Did he dislike you?

ROBERT. I think he was satisfied with my work. That was all he required of an employee. He didn't need our friendship.

BAXTER (*moving above the armchair*) You were his accountant. I suppose he'd no reason to mistrust you?

ROBERT. All my books are examined by auditors, Superintendent.

BAXTER. Do you know *Mrs* Marshall well?

ROBERT. What? (*He is puzzled. He suddenly laughs*) Oh, I see. (*To Marian*) You told him.

MARIAN. Yes, I did.

ROBERT (*to Baxter*) Miss Selby quite mistakenly believes I am having an affair with Mrs Marshall. She accused me of it several days ago. (*Rising and moving to* L *of Baxter*)

MARIAN (*rising*) Of course it's true! You know perfectly well it's true.

ROBERT. She also had curious delusions about her employer. He inspired in her a maternal urge to protect him. So when Mrs Marshall made a point of stopping in my office for a chat, Miss Selby suspected the worst.

BAXTER (*to Marian*) What reason had you, Miss Selby?

MARIAN. *Mr Marshall* told me so.

ROBERT. He—what?

MARIAN. Told me so.

ROBERT (C) Look. I was *not* having an affair with Mrs Marshall!

(CLAIRE *enters down* R)

CLAIRE. I think I should add my denial to Mr Westerby's.

BAXTER. Sit down, Mrs Marshall.

MRS PIPER. Yes, dear, come and sit down.

(CLAIRE *sits in the armchair.* MARIAN *sits down* L)

ROBERT. And, even if it had been true, I don't see any . . . (*He *pauses*) Oh, I see, you suggest I'm in love with Mrs Marshall, so I killed her husband to get him out of the way. Is that it?

BAXTER. You haven't been accused of anything.

MRS PIPER (*rising*) Not yet! (*She crosses to* R *of the door up* C)

(*As* CLAIRE *speaks*, BAXTER *moves to* L *of her*)

CLAIRE. I think I can explain, Superintendent. My husband did believe it was true of Mr Westerby and me. He was rather annoyed because we enjoyed each other's company.

BAXTER. But that's all it was?

(ROBERT *sits at the table* R *and lights a cigarette*)

CLAIRE. I like Mr Westerby immensely. I'm sure he feels the same way about me.

BAXTER. But your husband thought it went deeper than that.

CLAIRE. Oh, yes, he accused me of it.

BAXTER. Without reason?

CLAIRE. He had a reason, but it was not justified. He went to extreme lengths to prove himself right. He even hired a private detective to follow me whenever I left the house.

BAXTER. Did he indeed?

CLAIRE. Yes.

MRS PIPER. I'm glad you told him that. It comes better from you than me.

BAXTER. You mean—(*moving* LC) you knew about it?

MRS PIPER. Oh, yes. Well, I mean I just happened to see it on a sheet of paper at the back of a book in a drawer inside his desk. The Open-Eye Enquiry Agency.

(MARIAN *rises and moves up to above the desk*)

But I could see something was going on with my eyes shut.

BAXTER (*turning back*) And what *was* going on, Mrs Marshall?

CLAIRE (*with a sigh*) Not murder, Superintendent. They told my husband that I was visiting Mr Westerby's flat in St John's Wood.

BAXTER. Why should they say that if it wasn't true?

CLAIRE. It was true.

BAXTER. I see.

CLAIRE. But—I didn't go there to meet Mr Westerby.

BAXTER. You mean—there was someone else?

CLAIRE. Yes.

BAXTER (*to Claire, moving above to* R *of her chair*) What you're saying is that Mr Westerby, your husband's employee, was persuaded to let you meet another man in his rooms?

CLAIRE. It sounds sordid, doesn't it?

BAXTER. I'm not concerned with morals, Mrs Marshall, just facts. So your husband suspected Mr Westerby. Is that it?

CLAIRE. Yes! Yes, I told you he did! (*She rises and moves to the desk for a cigarette*)

BAXTER (*to Robert*) What's your comment on that?
ROBERT. It's true, of course. (*He rises and moves down* R)

(MARIAN *moves to up* R *of the desk*)

BAXTER. Did Mr Marshall accuse you of being his wife's lover?
ROBERT (*nodding*) Without the slightest hesitation.
BAXTER. Did you explain the true facts to him?
ROBERT. I did not. (*He crosses below to light Claire's cigarette*) Mrs
Marshall and I happen to share an interest in old prints. I said
she'd visited me two or three times.

(CLAIRE *moves to* L *of the desk*)

MRS PIPER. To look at 'is etchings.

(CLAIRE *turns and looks at Mrs Piper*)

BAXTER. Did he believe you?
ROBERT (*shaking his head*) No.
BAXTER. Was he content to continue as your employer?
ROBERT. You mean—did he sack me? His business was more
important than his marriage. He might have got round to it eventu-
ally. (*He moves* L *of Baxter*) Even so, I didn't kill him.
MARIAN (*at* R *end of the desk*) But you sympathize with whoever
did!
ROBERT. It shouldn't have gone to that extreme. Not even with
Marshall.
BAXTER. You must have made the acquaintance of Mrs Marshall's
friend?
ROBERT. At my flat? Oddly enough I didn't.
BAXTER. You never saw him?
ROBERT. No.
MARIAN. He went out like a little gentleman.
ROBERT. I gave Mrs Marshall a key.
BAXTER (*crossing below to Claire*) Mrs Marshall. (*He offers her a
sheet of notepaper*) I wonder if you'd write down the name of your
friend on this sheet of paper?

(ROBERT *moves to above the armchair*)

MRS PIPER. 'Ere's a pencil, dear. (*She feels in her pocket*)
CLAIRE. I'm afraid I can't do that.
BAXTER. Why not?
CLAIRE. I see no reason why I should. (*She moves away* L)
BAXTER. Very well. We'll leave it there for the moment. Later I
might have to insist.

(GODDARD *enters up* C)

GODDARD. The typist, sir. Victoria Reynolds.

(ROBERT *moves to sit below the table* R, *in his own time*)

BAXTER. Show her in. (*Moving to the table* R *and putting the pad on it*)
GODDARD (*standing* L *in the doorway*) Will you come this way,
please, Miss Reynolds?

(VICKIE *enters up* C. GODDARD *exits, closing the door.* BAXTER
stands R, *checking his watch,* MRS PIPER *meets Vickie and they come* C,
both talking about the murder excitedly. BAXTER *coughs.* MRS PIPER *says*
"*Ssh!*" *and sits in the chair* R *of the desk.* VICKIE *stands* R *of her.*
BAXTER *crosses to* R *of Vickie*)

BAXTER. Miss Reynolds, you obviously know why we are here?
VICKIE. Oh, yes, and it's no surprise to me.
BAXTER. What isn't?
VICKIE. That somebody bumped him off. I told Mrs Piper. (*To
Mrs Piper*) Do you remember, love? (*To Baxter*) I said if he didn't
stop laying his hands on me I'd hit him with the first thing I could
pick up. (*She stops as* MRS PIPER *nudges her, turns and sees Claire*) Oh,
Mrs Marshall, I didn't know you were there! I'm so sorry.
BAXTER. He made advances to you?
VICKIE. Well, he tried to.
MARIAN (*moving round* L *of the desk to below it*) It's a lie.
VICKIE. A lie? (*To Mrs Piper*) Is it true? Did I say it?
MRS PIPER. That's right, she did.
VICKIE (*giggling; to Baxter*) She saw him. She came in and saw
him.
MARIAN (L *of Mrs Piper*) Once. Just once. (*She moves down* L *and
faces* L) It was a misunderstanding.
VICKIE. I didn't misunderstand it. (*To Baxter*) She happened to
come in when he had his arms round me. She burst into tears. Then
she picked up that knife from his desk. This one. (*She picks it up,
above Mrs Piper*) For a minute I thought . . . (*She moves back to* L *of
Baxter*)
BAXTER. Yes?
VICKIE. Well, if looks could kill!
MARIAN (*turning*) Did you say "kill"?
VICKIE. I didn't mean . . .
MARIAN. You said "kill".
VICKIE. It was just an expression.
MARIAN (*moving in and speaking across Mrs Piper*) Are you suggesting
I killed him?
VICKIE. Oh, of course I didn't! Don't be such a misery!
MRS PIPER (*rising and leading Vickie to the armchair*) Now, girls,
girls . . . (*She stands* L *of Vickie*)

(VICKIE *sits in the armchair*)

MARIAN. Really, Superintendent, I must protest at these wild
accusations.
BAXTER. Miss Reynolds was merely demonstrating that you

might have done it. In fact any one of you might have done it. In my opinion the murderer is here in this office now.

MRS PIPER (*after a pause in which they all look at each other*) Well, of course, I wouldn't want to speak out of turn . . .

BAXTER. Then don't!

MRS PIPER. But that knife she's holding in her hand—that's the one that killed him.

(VICKIE *throws the knife down and runs down* R *to below Robert.* MRS PIPER *picks it up*)

That's it all right. I saw it when I found the body.

(BAXTER *moves to* R *of her and takes it*)

Mind out for the fingerprints, dear, you'll wipe off the evidence.

ROBERT. Did *you* find the body? Where?

MRS PIPER. In Mr Logan's office. Then I come in here to telephone, and there it was—in here!

ROBERT. What do you mean—there it was, in here!

BAXTER (*moving above the armchair*) You seem interested, Mr Westerby. Mrs Piper telephoned to say the body was in here. When we arrived it had gone.

ROBERT. I never heard such a thing in my life.

BAXTER (*to* L *of Robert*) I'm older than you. Neither did I.

MARIAN (*moving in to* L *of the armchair*) Superintendent, may I offer a word of advice? Insist on Mrs Marshall's telling you the name of her lover.

ROBERT (*rising*) Will you stop being a bitch for once?

CLAIRE. Robert, don't bother, she's hysterical.

MARIAN. It might turn out to be Mr Westerby after all.

(ROBERT *moves angrily to Marian, then crosses below to* L *of her, shouting. Everyone starts arguing.* VICKIE *moves up stage and puts her bag on the desk*)

BAXTER. Quiet! Let's have order! Quiet! Will you all, please, sit down?

(MARIAN *and* MRS PIPER *both attempt to sit on the chair* C, *and collide.* MRS PIPER *laughs and sits in the armchair.* MARIAN *sits in the chair* C. CLAIRE *sits down* L. VICKIE *sits on the* R *arm of the armchair.* ROBERT *moves to the desk and sits on the edge of the* L *side*)

BAXTER. I must insist on no more outbursts until I've finished my inquiries.

(MRS PIPER *turns to Vickie*)

Or interruptions.

MRS PIPER. Well, I wasn't saying anything. It's always *me*.

BAXTER. Somebody murdered Richard Marshall with this weapon. You, Miss Selby? (*He moves to* R *of Marian*)

MARIAN. No!

BAXTER. In a fit of jealousy? You loved him. What is it they say about a woman scorned?

MRS PIPER. "Hell hath no . . . !"

BAXTER (*turning to* L *of her*) I know! Or you, Mrs Piper, smarting under the supposed injustice of your husband's dismissal? Was it you?

MRS PIPER. If I murdered everybody who sacked Fred I'd need a machine-gun, not a paper-knife.

(BAXTER, *proud of his mastery of the situation, paces the room, crossing to down* R)

BAXTER (*to Claire*) Or you, Mrs Marshall? You loved another man. (*Crossing* L) Did you rid yourself of Richard Marshall to clear the path for your real love? (*Quickly turning to Robert*) Or you, Mr Westerby? Is your story true? Or are you indeed the lover of Claire Marshall? (*He stands* L *of the desk*)

ROBERT. No!

(*There is silence*)

MRS PIPER. Ooh! Isn't it dramatic? (*She rises and moves below the desk* C *to put the knife on it*)

(GODDARD *enters up* C)

GODDARD. Superintendent! Sir . . .

BAXTER. I don't wish to be disturbed.

GODDARD. But, sir . . .

BAXTER. I said I don't wish to be disturbed.

GODDARD. Yes, sir, but . . . (*Backing to the door, he points up stage*)

BAXTER. Unless, of course . . . Have you found Marshall's body?

GODDARD. Yes, sir. (*He hesitates*) I suppose you *could* put it like that. (*He stands* R *of the door*)

(RICHARD MARSHALL *comes in to* C)

MARSHALL. What is going on here? What is everybody doing in my private office?

MRS PIPER. It's the boss! It's Mr Marshall.

CURTAIN

ACT II

SCENE—*The same. About six o'clock the following evening.*

When the CURTAIN *rises,* MRS PIPER *is seated in the armchair reading the "Evening Standard". With her left hand she pushes a Hoover cleaner to and fro.* VICKIE *enters up* C *with her coat on, and carrying an umbrella. She pretends to stab Mrs Piper in the back.* MRS PIPER *rises, moves up* C *and hits Vickie with the newspaper)*

MRS PIPER. I've had a bad enough day without your making it worse.

VICKIE (R *of her; laughing)* I laugh every time I think about it.

MRS PIPER. One of these days the truth will come out. I've been thinking. *(She takes off her glasses, puts them in their case and into her apron)*

VICKIE. The Superintendent said you'd been drinking. What was it he called you—the Pie-Eyed Piper of Hamelin?

MRS PIPER. It's all very well for you to laugh, but I spoke the truth. He was dead. Without a word of a lie. Believe me. *(She moves to the desk and puts the paper on it* C)

VICKIE. We did until he came in—alive.

(MRS PIPER takes the Hoover to L *of the table down* R, *unplugs it, and picks up her bucket from* L *of the table.*
ROBERT WESTERBY enters down R. *He grins at Mrs Piper. He is carrying a file, a briefcase and his coat.* VICKIE *sits on the* L *arm of the armchair)*

ROBERT *(singing)* "I—ain't got no bo-dy . . ." *(He puts the file on the* R *end of the table)* It was a shame.

MRS PIPER. Go on, laugh! Silly things! Don't bother me, I put it down to ignorance. *(She moves up stage and puts the bucket on the floor at the up* R *end of the desk)*

ROBERT. Never mind, Mrs Piper, you cheered me up no end. Pity you were mistaken. *(He moves to* L *of the table and puts the briefcase on it)*

MRS PIPER. I never was. *(She takes out her duster and starts dusting the desk)*

ROBERT *(crossing above the armchair to* C) Oh, come now!

VICKIE. Old Baxter was a bit hard on you but, after all, love, you can't say you weren't mistaken.

(MRS PIPER picks up and dusts the empty ashtray)

ROBERT. You did make a fool of him, you know.

MRS PIPER. Nothing to what he made of me. (*She crosses to* L *of Robert*) When I told Fred what he'd said he was vivid. He said nobody'd a right to be offensive to me. Except 'im. (*Crosses back to the downstage end of the desk and replaces the ashtray*)

ROBERT (*standing* L *of Vickie, putting on his coat*) We certainly learned a few home-truths about each other, eh, Vickie?

VICKIE. We found out who was who's.

(MRS PIPER, *dusting the desk, slowly works* L *of it to the upstage end*)

I thought it was dreadful of Miss Selby to suggest you were having an affair with Mrs Marshall. The very idea!

ROBERT. Oh, the idea was all right.

VICKIE. Was it?

ROBERT. She's very attractive. (*He sighs*) Unfortunately it didn't happen to be true. I'm off. (*Crossing to pick up his briefcase*) Don't let it get you down, Mrs Piper.

MRS PIPER. Nothing keeps me down for long.

ROBERT (*crossing back to up* C) Remember that we still love you—whatever the Superintendent says.

MRS PIPER. 'Ere, tell me one thing, Mr Westerby. (*She moves above the desk to* L *of* ROBERT)

ROBERT. Yes?

MRS PIPER. There was blood on the chair. 'Course, it could 'ave been mine or 'Arry's—banging the chair like mad. 'Ere, haven't they got some new-fangled way of telling whose blood it is?

ROBERT. Yes, I can't pretend to know much about it but, as far as I remember, there are four blood groups. Each of us belongs to one of the four.

MRS PIPER. Oh! Then the experts would know whose it was?

ROBERT. No, they wouldn't know whose it was. They'd know whose it wasn't.

MRS PIPER. It's beyond me.

ROBERT. One group is rare, the others more common.

MRS PIPER. Isn't it marvellous!

ROBERT. We live in a wonderful world, Mrs Piper. (*He kisses her*) Good night! 'Night, Vickie.

VICKIE. Good night, Mr Westerby.

(ROBERT *exits up* C, *closing the door*)

Isn't he fab?

MRS PIPER (*moving down stage*) *What* did he say? If it wasn't our blood they'd know?

VICKIE. Oh, forget it! (*She rises and moves* R *of Mrs Piper*)

MRS PIPER. I was a blood donor once. They gave me a ticket and a cup of tea. I wonder what I did with it.

VICKIE. Drank it, I expect.

MRS PIPER. No, I mean the ticket with my blood group on. I wonder if 'Arry's got one? No, 'e'd give somebody blood poisoning, 'e would. (*She crosses* R *below Vickie, puts her duster on the table, and starts winding up the Hoover flex*)

VICKIE. I'm going home. I thought we were getting the day off, didn't you? The boss *would* come in and spoil everything!

MRS PIPER (*moving in to her*) Vickie, I'm going to prove I'm right. I knew Baxter when he wore short pants. We was mixed infants at Benson Street Primary School—great mottled knees he had. I'll show him. Vickie, I've been reading the *Evening Standard* . . .

VICKIE. Tell me tomorrow, love. I'll miss my bus. (*She moves up* C)

MRS PIPER. No, Vickie. There's an article . . .

(VICKIE *opens the door up* C, RICHARD MARSHALL *comes in*)

MARSHALL (R *of Vickie*) Which bus, Miss Reynolds?

VICKIE. It's after six o'clock.

MARSHALL. Has Miss Selby gone?

MRS PIPER. Yes, sir.

(MARSHALL *crosses to* L *of Vickie, opens his briefcase and hands her some paper.* MRS PIPER *leaves her duster on the* R *end of the table, moves up to close the* C *door, picks up her carrier bag from the chair up* R, *puts it on the floor down* R *of the table, and takes out a bottle and some rags*)

MARSHALL. These papers must be posted tonight. The addresses are on them.

VICKIE. Well, I . . .

MARSHALL. It'll only take you five minutes.

VICKIE. I suppose I can spare five. (*She goes down* R *with the papers*)

(MARSHALL *crosses above desk to* L *of it*)

MARSHALL. Oh, Miss Reynolds, there's a letter here for signature. Come back for it.

(VICKIE *exits down* R)

Don't like work nowadays, do they—the younger generation? (*He puts his hat and briefcase on the up* R *end of the desk*)

MRS PIPER. No, sir. (*Shaking the bottle and damping the cloth*) That's right, sir.

MARSHALL. All the things that were said yesterday won't help with discipline. A lot of dirty washing was on display—so I'm told. (*He puts on his glasses*)

MRS PIPER. Yes, sir.

MARSHALL. Most unfortunate. (*He sees the paper on the desk*) And most mysterious. Carry on with what you're doing, Mrs Piper. You won't disturb me.

(MRS PIPER *is watching him thoughtfully*)

MRS PIPER. Yes, sir.

MARSHALL. I said—you can get on. (*He pockets the paper and sits at the desk*)

MRS PIPER. Thank you, sir. (*She moves to the desk and puts the bottle on the* R *end of it*) They said they was bringing the chair back today, but they haven't yet. (*She kneels*)

MARSHALL. Chair? (*He reads the letter awaiting signature*)

MRS PIPER. With the blood on it. (*She rubs the desk, shaking it*)

MARSHALL. Perhaps they'll deliver it tomorrow. (*He signs the letter*) Look, can't you operate somewhere else whilst I'm here?

MRS PIPER (*moving away*) Oh, I beg your pardon, sir! It's a special embrocation for the legs. I'm sorry if I shook the desk. I'm a bit shook up myself today, sir.

MARSHALL. You need a holiday. (*He puts the letter on the desk*)

MRS PIPER. That's what I keep telling Fred. He says we spent a fortnight at Brighton in August.

MARSHALL (*drawing on the jotter pad*) And did you?

MRS PIPER. Yes. Three years ago. There's some funny things going on round 'ere, Mr Marshall. (*She looks under the rug*)

MARSHALL. Yes, I dare say. (*He sees her on her hands and knees looking under the rug and looks over at her*) What on earth are you doing down there?

MRS PIPER. Searching.

MARSHALL. Have you lost something?

MRS PIPER. Yes, I have—my reputation. That's what I've lost.

MARSHALL. You won't find it down there!

MRS PIPER. I don't know what I'll find. (*She rises, taking out some keys from her pocket*) I found these keys down the back of a chair in Mr Logan's office. Whose do you suppose they are?

MARSHALL (*taking off his glasses and leaving them on the desk*) I really don't know, Mrs Piper. As far as I'm concerned the matter has now been dropped.

MRS PIPER. Not by me it hasn't.

MARSHALL (*rising and moving below the desk to* L *of Mrs Piper*) May I look at the keys?

MRS PIPER. No name on it. Just initials. J.P.G.

MARSHALL. I don't know anyone with those initials. But, Mrs Piper, you don't still think I'm dead, do you?

MRS PIPER. I think you were last night.

MARSHALL. That's rather silly, isn't it?

MRS PIPER (*grudgingly*) I suppose so. It doesn't make sense.

MARSHALL. Of course it doesn't. (*Amiably*) You must have made a mistake.

MRS PIPER. I've made a lot in my time. But if I made this one I must be going round the twist. (*She picks up her bottle and rags and puts them in the bag down* R. *Then she continues winding up the Hoover flex*)

MARSHALL. You know. I've been thinking. (*He picks up his hat and briefcase, and crosses up* C) You're a valuable member of our organization. I shouldn't like to lose you. Your husband—tell him he can start work again tomorrow. How does that please you?

MRS PIPER. It pleases me more than it'll please him.

MARSHALL (*at the door*) There we are, then! Good night!

MRS PIPER. Good night, sir!

MARSHALL. Oh . . . (*He goes back to her*) Perhaps *I'd* better have those keys. I'll check with the rest of the staff tomorrow.

MRS PIPER. I've already checked—*today.*

MARSHALL. Oh! I wonder if they're mine?

MRS PIPER. J.P.G.?

MARSHALL. No, they can't be, can they?

MRS PIPER. No, sir. Good night, sir. (*She puts the Hoover above the door down* R *and picks up the duster*)

MARSHALL. Good night! (*He hesitates*) What *are* you going to do with them?

MRS PIPER. Well, I had thought of handing them over to the police.

MARSHALL (*moving to* L *of her*) I shouldn't if I were you. I can just imagine what Baxter will say. (*Loudly, in imitation*) "A bunch of keys! Is that all?"

MRS PIPER. Yes, I expect he would. Sarky hound!

MARSHALL (*moving up stage*) Well, there you are!

MRS PIPER. But that *isn't* all.

MARSHALL. It isn't?

MRS PIPER. No, sir.

MARSHALL. Do you mean you've made another discovery?

MRS PIPER. Yes, sir. A button. This one, sir. (*She displays it*)

(MARSHALL *moves to* L *of her*)

I never seen one like it before. All fancy colours on it like a seashell. That's very dainty, ain't it?

MARSHALL. Where did you find that?

MRS PIPER (*meaningfully*) Down 'ere. (*She crosses below the armchair to* LC) Where the chair would be if it was.

MARSHALL (*following above the armchair to up* R *of her*) Are you thinking of reporting this to the police?

MRS PIPER. Yes, I think so, sir.

MARSHALL. Why? All the evidence in the world won't convince them that I was murdered last night.

MRS PIPER. I suppose I'm being foolish.

MARSHALL (*backing up stage*) Of course you are!

MRS PIPER. He'd laugh at me.

MARSHALL. Of course he would!

MRS PIPER. Perhaps I shouldn't bother him after all.

MARSHALL (*at the door up* C) Of course you shouldn't!

MRS PIPER. I think I will, though.

MARSHALL (*moving down to her*) I'll tell you what I'll do. I happen to know the Superintendent personally. Give them to me and I'll slip round and show them to him.

MRS PIPER. That's a very good idea, sir.

MARSHALL. Good!

MRS PIPER. But I couldn't put you to all that trouble.

MARSHALL. It's no trouble at all.

MRS PIPER. No, sir, p'raps I *ought* to think it over again. I'll put them in my pocket and 'ang on to them for the time being. (*She turns her back on him, raises her skirt, and puts the keys in a pocket hidden from view*)

(MARSHALL *moves down to watch her*)

There we are, sir. Deep in the heart of Texas. (*She moves round below the desk to above* C *of it*) I'd better get on with my work, else I *shall* get drummed out of the Brownies.

MARSHALL. Yes, well—very well.

MRS PIPER. Good night, sir. (*She picks up the ashtray*)

MARSHALL. Good night.

(MARSHALL *exits up* C. MRS PIPER *empties the ashtray into the tin and as she resets it finds the piece of paper Marshall was doodling on. She tears it off the pad.* VICKIE *enters* R. MRS PIPER *puts the paper down her dress*)

VICKIE. Has he gone home?

MRS PIPER. Yes.

VICKIE (*moving to the desk*) And that's where I'm going, too. Where's that letter? (*She picks up the letter and envelope and moves to* C, *putting the letter inside*) Well, so long! Don't do anything I wouldn't do!

MRS PIPER. There *isn't* anything.

(VICKIE *moves to the door up* C. MRS PIPER *follows to* L *of her*)

'Ere, you're just the one I want to see . . .

VICKIE. I'm in a hurry. My friend and I are meeting a couple of boys.

MRS PIPER. Their business can wait. (*She pushes her to the chair at the table down* R) Mine can't. Be a darling, Vickie, sit down and type a letter for me.

VICKIE. Oh, I'm tired. I've worked an eight-hour day.

MRS PIPER. You haven't worked eight hours in your life. Not if you added it all up. Do as you're told. It's important.

VICKIE. Oh, you are a nuisance! Who's it to? (*She sits at the table down* R, *putting down her bag and letter, and picks up a notepad and pencil*)

MRS PIPER (L *of Vickie*) Superintendent Baxter.

VICKIE (*rising*) Oh, no. I'm not having anything to do with *him*.

MRS PIPER. I will be responsible. (*She pushes her down*)

VICKIE (*sitting again and giggling*) You do stick your neck out, don't you?

MRS PIPER. "Dear 'Arry."

VICKIE. *Dear* Harry?

MRS PIPER. You just put what I tell you to. "Dear 'Arry. I suppose you thought you was very clever this morning?" Question mark. "Well, I'm not so daft neither." Full stop.

VICKIE. Will you say that again?

MRS PIPER. Take a letter, Miss Reynolds. (*She moves to* R *of the armchair*) It may interest you to know—my stockings is all twisted up—that I have discovered two vital clues. (*She sits on the* R *arm of the armchair*)

VICKIE. What sort of clues?

MRS PIPER. I'm not telling *you*. One, a bunch of keys owned by an unknown owner. Two, a waistcoat button off a waistcoat shaped like a seashell. Have you got that, Vickie?

VICKIE. Yes.

MRS PIPER. Have you read the evening papers?

VICKIE. Look, I haven't had time yet.

MRS PIPER. No, that's in the letter, you flaming fool.

(VICKIE *puts down the pad and pencil and rises to* R *of Mrs Piper*)

VICKIE. Wouldn't it be quicker to telephone? Do you know his private number?

MRS PIPER. It's Victoria eight-nine-seven-five. But I'd rather have wrote 'im a letter.

VICKIE. Let's get it done with. (*She moves to the phone down* R *and dials the number*)

MRS PIPER. 'Ere, when he comes on, ask him if he's read the evening paper.

VICKIE. You ask him.

MRS PIPER. I'm deaf in one ear on the phone.

VICKIE. Ssshh! (*Into the phone*) Hello! Superintendent Baxter? . . . Hold the line, please, I have a call for you. An old friend wishes to speak to you. A Mrs Piper. (*She gasps and bursts out laughing*)

MRS PIPER (*rising*) 'Ere, give it to me! (*She crosses below Vickie and takes the phone*)

(VICKIE *stands facing her above the armchair*)

'Ere, listen to me, Clever Clogs! Have you read the evening paper? Because there's been an anonymous corpse picked up dead at Notting Hill. And I'm asking you to find out if there's a button missing off the waistcoat. 'Cause if there is I've got it. And, kindly ascertain, is 'is blood group the same as the blood on the chair? And if he's lost his keys—I've got them, too. (*She hangs up suddenly, moves up stage, picks up the bucket, and returns to* R *of Vickie*) That'll spoil his supper.

VICKIE. I wouldn't like to be you if you've dragged him out of bed again for nothing.

MRS PIPER. Vickie, I saw what I saw.

VICKIE. But you said it was the boss.

MRS PIPER. I said it was the boss in this office. I didn't say who was in the other. I didn't look at him close.

VICKIE. You just said yourself there couldn't be two of them.

MRS PIPER (*moving down* R *and putting the bucket on the floor above the door*) I'm not saying I'm happy about it, am I?

VICKIE (*moving to pick up the letter from the table* R) Well, I hope the Superintendent is. I'm off before he gets here.

MRS PIPER. I don't care about him. If he comes, it means I've hit the nail on the head.

VICKIE. He'll probably treat you the same way. (*She moves to* L *of her, sealing the envelope*)

MRS PIPER. 'Ere, Vickie, I'm not sure I'm safe to be left alone.

VICKIE. That's what I'm beginning to think.

MRS PIPER. I mean, perhaps my *life's* in danger. Perhaps I *know* too much. 'Ere, you'd better stay until Baxter arrives.

VICKIE (*impressed*) You're really frightened, aren't you? Are you sure you weren't fuzzy last night?

MRS PIPER. It takes more than a couple of mild-and-bitters to affect my eyesight.

(*There are several grim and portentous knocks on the door up* C. *They react nervously*)

VICKIE. Oh!

MRS PIPER. Someone's knocking at the door.

VICKIE. I know.

MRS PIPER (*pushing her upstage*) You'd better see who it is.

VICKIE (*pulling her*) *You* see who it is.

MRS PIPER (*pulling away*) I don't particularly want to know.

(*The knocks are repeated*)

VICKIE. Oh, all right then! (*She opens the door*)

(GODDARD *enters with the chair over his head*)

GODDARD. Good evening! I've brought the chair back.

(VICKIE *closes the door*)

Where does it go?

(MRS PIPER *indicates the position of the tub chair, below the upstage end of the desk*)

MRS PIPER. You know where it goes. Standing there gawping at our Vickie! (*She moves to* LC *below the desk*) I seen your Adam's apple working overtime.

(VICKIE, *impressed by Goddard, is less eager to leave.* GODDARD *places the chair in its original position*)

VICKIE. Fancy sending you with it!

GODDARD (*to Vickie*) I volunteered. How are you, Mrs Piper? The Superintendent's in a better humour now. He's back in bed with a nice hot-water bottle.

MRS PIPER. I hope it bursts.

VICKIE. He's on his way here. She's sent for him again.

GODDARD. She's—what?

VICKIE. She's discovered fresh evidence.

GODDARD (*moving to* R *of Mrs Piper*) Do you mean Mr Marshall is *really* dead this time?

MRS PIPER. My information is for the Super's ears—not his underlings. (*Crossing below to down* R) You may abscond.

GODDARD. I think I'll stay and watch the fun.

MRS PIPER (*picking up her brush and duster*) Oh, very crisp! I say! (*She turns*) Did your so-called experts examine the chair for blood-stains?

GODDARD. I don't suppose they bothered after they learned Mr Marshall was still alive.

MRS PIPER. That's something I shall discuss when I'm in camera with the Super.

VICKIE (*to Goddard*) Time I was off. (*She moves up stage*)

GODDARD. Yes. (*He follows her*)

MRS PIPER (*crossing above the armchair and below Vickie to between her and Goddard*) I say, young fellow—Vickie and me have been arguing. Can a man be killed in one place and his body be found in another?

GODDARD. I suppose so, if he was moved.

MRS PIPER. In other words, I might see him here and the police might see him in Notting Hill?

GODDARD. Yes.

(MRS PIPER *turns triumphantly to Vickie*)

VICKIE. But if you did, love, he wouldn't come walking in at the door a few hours later. (*To Goddard*) Would he?

GODDARD. It's never happened before.

VICKIE. Besides, you were in the building all the time. You'd have seen him.

MRS PIPER. Not if he'd used the fire-escape. Look here. (*She crosses* L *to the fire exit*)

(GODDARD *follows to* R *of the desk*, VICKIE *to* R *of Goddard*)

Through this door over the flat roof and down the service stairs.

GODDARD. Is this fresh evidence, Mrs Piper, or theories?

MRS PIPER. Oh, I don't know! My hubby and I talked it over until we both got the jaw-ache. It's the keys he thinks are important. He says Baxter will really get excited when I show him the keys.

GODDARD. Which keys?

MRS PIPER (*moving to below the desk*) Turn around and I'll show you.

GODDARD. Turn round?

MRS PIPER. Turn round.

(VICKIE *and* GODDARD, *smiling at each other, turn away*. MRS PIPER *raises her skirt and fumbles until she finds the keys*)

(*Laughing*) I tickled myself.

(*They turn*)

I found these at the back of the chair in Mr Logan's office. Perhaps you can can tell me how they got there, and whose they are?

GODDARD (*moving below the desk to her*) They're mine. (*He takes them*)

MRS PIPER (*stepping back in alarm*) Yours?

GODDARD. I assure you, I didn't murder anybody.

VICKIE. How could *you* lose them in there?

GODDARD. They must have fallen out of my pocket. When I was searching the room, I suppose. Look (*to Vickie*) my initials are on them. J.P.G. Jeremy Patterson Goddard.

VICKIE (*delighted*) Oh! Is your name Jeremy? How fab!

MRS PIPER. 'Ere, are you sure?

GODDARD. It's what I've always been called.

MRS PIPER (*to Vickie*) Whatever will Baxter say?

GODDARD. I don't know how to thank you. (*He puts the keys in his jacket pocket*)

MRS PIPER (*crossing below the armchair*) He will!

GODDARD. Oh, lord! That was your evidence, wasn't it?

MRS PIPER. I'll hang on to the button if there's an earthquake. (*She sits in the armchair*)

GODDARD. Button?

VICKIE. She found it on the floor.

GODDARD. May I see it?

MRS PIPER. If you do you'll say it came off your trousers. I'd better keep *something* to show 'im when he gets here.

VICKIE (*to Goddard*) I really must go.

GODDARD. Me, too.

VICKIE. Are you off duty?

GODDARD. I wish I were.

VICKIE. Pity. Perhaps we can ride in the lift together. (*To Mrs Piper*) Good night, love. Try not to worry. (*To Goddard*) There are some papers in Mr Westerby's office I have to post. Will you wait for me?

GODDARD. I'll come with you. (*He crosses below the armchair to open the door down R*)

VICKIE. Oh! Thank you. (*She moves to the door down R*)

MRS PIPER. Vickie! Vickie!

(VICKIE *returns to* R *of Mrs Piper*)

Beware the long arm of the law!

VICKIE. It won't take a minute.

MRS PIPER. Telling me!

(VICKIE *moves to the door and exits down* R. GODDARD *follows, closing the door.* MRS PIPER *rises and moves to clean the chair* R *of the desk. She has her back to the door c when the door begins slowly to open. It creaks ominously and she faces forward, stiffens anxiously, then turns quickly. As she does so the door closes quickly but soundlessly. She continues with her work and the door begins to open again. A hand reaches into the room and switches off the lights. The office is in complete darkness. We hear the sound of a scuffle, and* MRS PIPER'S *protestations. After a pause, during which she calls "Help!" the door down* R *opens.* GODDARD *comes in, switching on the lights from down* R. VICKIE *follows him.* MRS PIPER *revealed lying on floor legs up on the tub chair which is overturned)*

GODDARD (R *of Mrs Piper*) Are you all right?
MRS PIPER. Help!

(GODDARD *helps her up*)

VICKIE. We're here. What's the matter? (*She crosses to below* L *of her*)
GODDARD. Is something wrong? (*He replaces the chair*)
MRS PIPER (*sitting in the chair*) Help! Follow that man. Quick!
VICKIE. Which man? (*She hands Mrs Piper her brush*)
MRS PIPER. Any man. He switched the lights off and took me unawares.
GODDARD. Took you what?
MRS PIPER. Never you mind. I've been assaulted. Well, *do* something!
GODDARD. Yes, well—right . . .

(GODDARD *exits quickly but vaguely up* C)

VICKIE. What did he do? (*She crosses above to* R *of Mrs Piper*)
MRS PIPER. He rolled me over on the floor.
VICKIE. What for?
MRS PIPER. How do I know? Been twenty years ago I could have told you!
VICKIE. What happened?
MRS PIPER (*stifling a giggle*) I can't tell you. It was rude.
VICKIE. I wonder who he was.
MRS PIPER (*almost sighing*) So do I.

(GODDARD *enters up* C, *closing the door, and moves to* R *of Vickie*)

GODDARD. Mrs Piper, were you *really* attacked? There's no sign of anybody.
MRS PIPER. Of course I was attacked. I don't *imagine* things and *tell* people they happened.
GODDARD. Well, it's very odd.
MRS PIPER. It's never happened to me before. Not as quickly as that.
GODDARD. We were only gone for a few seconds.
MRS PIPER (*thinking hard*) 'Ere, just a minute! I wonder . . .
VICKIE. Now what?

Mrs Piper (*rising*) Turn round again. (*She moves* lc, *leaving the brush in the chair*)

Vickie. Oh, no!

(Vickie *and* Goddard *turn round resignedly.* Mrs Piper *lifts her skirt and fumbles in her pocket*)

Mrs Piper. I knew it! It's gone. I knew it had.

(*They turn to face her. She is so affected by the discovery of her loss that she forgets to lower her skirt*)

Vickie. What's gone this time?

Mrs Piper. Somebody's pinched me button. (*She lowers her skirt hastily*)

Goddard (*moving to* r *of her*) But that's impossible.

Mrs Piper. Oh, my gawd! What shall I say when Baxter gets here? (*She moves down* l)

Vickie. Do you mean to say all your evidence has gone—the stuff you got him out of bed for?

Mrs Piper (*sitting down* l) Oh, I'm in a *hell* of a mess!

Vickie. See you tomorrow. (*She hurries to the door up* c) Heavens, look at the time!

Mrs Piper. Hold on. Hold on!

(Vickie *stops*)

Who knew I had a pocket in my . . . who knew it was there? The boss! Mr Marshall, that's who! (*She rises*)

Goddard. Not Mr Marshall again?

Mrs Piper. He saw me *put* it in there.

Vickie (*moving down stage*) Everybody knows where your pocket is. It's the biggest joke in the office.

Goddard. Are you suggesting Mr. Marshall attacked you?

Mrs Piper. Can you think of a likelier explanation?

Goddard. *I* can't, Mrs Piper. Perhaps the Superintendent can.

Mrs Piper (*crossing below to down* r) Oh, gawd! When he comes in here blowing that great hooter of 'is, it sounds like an Atlantic liner lost in a fog.

(*There is the sound of doors slamming, and heavy footsteps*)

Goddard. Stand by for blasting!

(Baxter *enters quickly up* c. *He is, as Mrs Piper anticipated, blowing his nose loudly with a large handkerchief. He moves to* r *of the armchair. He points at Mrs Piper*)

Baxter. All right—show me! And it had better be good.

Vickie. Ta-ta!

(Vickie *exits quickly up* c, *closing the door.*
    Mrs Piper *tries to follow*)

BAXTER (*barring her way*) I'm waiting.

GODDARD. Good evening, sir.

MRS PIPER. Good evening, sir.

GODDARD. Are you feeling better now, sir?

MRS PIPER. Yes, are you feeling better, 'Arry?

(BAXTER *senses that something is amiss. He glances at each of them suspiciously*)

BAXTER (*moving above the armchair*) I shall assume, Constable, that this is a genuine inquiry after my health—and inform you I am worse. (*He moves down stage. To Mrs Piper*) You were saying . . . ?

MRS PIPER (*moving to R of him; desperately*) Look, 'Arry—it's no use beating about the mulberries, darling. It's gone.

(BAXTER *is exasperated, but controls himself*)

BAXTER (*icily; facing front*) Gone?

MRS PIPER. Yes, it 'as. All me lovely evidence.

BAXTER (*facing her*) Did you say—gone?

MRS PIPER. Yes, I did, 'Arry.

BAXTER (*crossing below her to R of the armchair; horribly quiet*) Oh, well—never mind! I wasn't doing anything in particular, was I? (*At the top of his voice*) Except lying in a warm bed with pneumonia which will probably carry me off to my grave.

MRS PIPER. Well, don't blame me!

BAXTER (*yelling*) Don't blame you? Who shall I blame?

MRS PIPER. It's just one of those things.

BAXTER. *Which* things?

MRS PIPER. If you'll stop yelling at me I'll explain.

BAXTER (*sweetly*) But do! Do! (*He moves down R*)

MRS PIPER. Oo, your disposition 'as become 'orrible! (*She sits on the L arm of the armchair*)

BAXTER (*R of the armchair*) If my nature has been soured, let me tell you that people like you have done nothing to sweeten it. (*Crossing to C*) This is the second time in twenty-four hours you have fetched me out of a warm bed, and when I get here—(*crossing back R*) what do you say? "It's gone, 'Arry." Gone where?

MRS PIPER. How do *I* know? Blow your nose!

(BAXTER *does so and crosses back to C, below the armchair*)

Is that the All Clear or the warbling sound?

BAXTER. Fifteen minutes ago I was in bed with a hot-water bottle and a thermometer in my mouth.

MRS PIPER. There's room for both. Did you try the onion cure?

BAXTER. No, I didn't. (*He turns to Goddard*) Goddard, keep watch outside the door. (*He moves L of the desk and above it*)

GODDARD. Yes, sir. (*He moves to the door up C*)

(BAXTER *sneezes*)

MRS PIPER. Bless you, sir.

(GODDARD *exits up* C, *closing the door*)

BAXTER (*sitting behind the desk and putting his hat on the* R *end*) Now, perhaps you would care to tell me your story. It will be something to do. Time hangs heavily on my hands.

MRS PIPER (*pulling the tub chair up to* R *of the desk, and moving above it to* R *of Baxter, taking the duster but leaving the brush in it*) I'll tell you, but you won't like it.

BAXTER. You told me you had discovered a bunch of keys and a button. Where are they?

MRS PIPER. I know where the keys are. Your young fella out there —he says they're his.

BAXTER. And the button?

MRS PIPER. You won't believe this, it was in my pocket.

BAXTER. Which pocket?

MRS PIPER. Never you mind. It was secreted on my person. (*She moves to* R *of the chair*) I was alone in here and suddenly the lights went out. A man came in and pinched it. (*She picks up the brush*)

BAXTER. Did you see him?

MRS PIPER. How could I when the lights were out? He rolled me on the floor and—(*she laughs at the memory*) oh, it *was* disgusting! Rolling on the floor at my age. Leave off! (*She sits on the chair* R *of the desk, extends her arm and squashes his hat*)

(BAXTER *snatches it and puts it on the* L *end*)

BAXTER. Describe the button to me.

MRS PIPER. It was about so big. (*She measures on her finger-nail*) Most of it was grey but the inside part was all different colours like a seashell.

BAXTER (*rising; excitedly*) That's it! That's it! (*He moves round the* L *end of the desk*)

MRS PIPER (*rising*) You believe me? (*She moves to* R *of him*) Then let me tell you something else. The boss, Mr Marshall, was in 'ere talking to me about it. And shall I tell you what I think? I think he's the one who snaffled it.

BAXTER. Why?

MRS PIPER. Because 'e acted peculiar. 'E didn't want me to show it to you. Said 'e'd do it.

BAXTER. But you retained it?

MRS PIPER. I did until the lights went out and somebody took advantage of me. I was so busy protecting my honour I clean forgot about me button.

BAXTER. Where was Goddard when this happened?

MRS PIPER. He was in the next office with young Vickie. (*She points down* R *with the brush*)

BAXTER. Oh, *was* he?

Mrs Piper. They'd only been gone about sixty seconds. It was all over in a flash. Worse luck. (*She sits* R *of the desk again*)
Baxter (*crossing to the door up* c *and calling*) Goddard!

(Goddard *enters to* R *of Baxter, closing the door*)

Goddard. Sir?
Baxter. While you were in the next office with Miss Reynolds, Mrs Piper was attacked. What happened?
Goddard. Oh! When she screamed I ran straight here, sir. The lights were out and she appeared to be distressed. I made a brief search, but I couldn't see anyone.
Baxter. Why did you make a *brief* search?
Goddard. Because—frankly—sir, I didn't believe her. I thought it was merely her imagination.
Baxter. Why?
Goddard. If you remember, sir, you yourself said she was not to be relied upon.
Mrs Piper. Sauce!
Goddard. I came to the conclusion that she was a paranoid schizophrene unable to distinguish between the shadow and the substance.
Mrs Piper (*to Baxter*) 'Ere. What's that mean?
Baxter. Gawd knows! (*To Goddard*) Get Willis on the phone.
Goddard. Yes, sir. (*He crosses above to the telephone on the desk and dials*)
Mrs Piper. 'Ere, are you 'aving me arrested, 'Arry?
Baxter. Not yet. (*He moves to* R *of Goddard*) The keys found by Mrs Piper—you claimed them. Are you sure they're your property?
Goddard (*displaying them*) No doubt about it, sir.
Baxter. Let's have a look at them. Same initials. What's the J for—John?
Goddard. Jeremy, sir.

(Baxter *pulls a face and hands back the keys*)

Mrs Piper. I think it's fab.
Goddard (*into the phone*) Superintendent Baxter for Inspector Willis. (*To Baxter*) You're through, sir.

(Baxter *takes the phone from* Goddard, *who moves above to up* R *of the desk.* Baxter *passes below to sit on the desk chair*)

Baxter. Willis . . . No, I'm not better . . . I know I ought to be in bed . . . Look, I've just received some rather curious information. That body that was picked up at Notting Hill—has it been identified yet? . . . James Cameron. Now, the waistcoat buttons were unusual, sea-shell shape and one was missing. Well, the person who reported the murder yesterday at Chatham House now says she's found a button which seems to match up . . . No, don't get excited, Willis, that's gone, too . . . Yes, the person who mislaid the body has now mislaid the button, ha! ha! ha! (*He laughs*)

(MRS PIPER *mimics him soundlessly. He looks at her. She brushes her skirt self-consciously*)

One other question, Willis. What was Cameron's blood group? . . . It *was?* (*He rises*) I'll come round to see you. By the way, I think this person, Mrs Piper, should have protection. An attempt might be made to remove her. (*He replaces the receiver and crosses behind Mrs Piper, taking his hat*)

MRS PIPER (*catching on to his coat*) 'Ere, who's going to remove me, 'Arry?

BAXTER. I don't know, I'm just hoping. (*He moves up* R, *taking off his coat*) Goddard!

GODDARD. Yes, sir?

BAXTER. Get downstairs and see if you can find Marshall. Tell him I want to see him.

GODDARD. Yes, sir.

(GODDARD *exits up* C, *closing the door.* BAXTER *puts his hat and coat on the chair up* R *and moves back to above the armchair*)

MRS PIPER. Fred always says: "Mind your own business and let other people mind theirs." But it don't seem to harmonize with my temperament. (*Rising and crossing to* L *of him*) What were you saying about 'is blood group, 'Arry?

BAXTER. He belonged to group AB. Very rare. Mine is O. Common.

MRS PIPER. Well, it would be, wouldn't it?

BAXTER. The blood on the chair was AB. The same as his.

MRS PIPER. Oo—then it *was* 'is!

BAXTER. It *could* be. The button might have been conclusive evidence if things ever stayed put in this place . . .

MRS PIPER. Well, it wasn't my fault if I was took advantage of.

BAXTER (*moving down* R) I'll take another look around in there. I'm probably wasting my time. The fingerprint boys only found one identifiable set of prints. *They* were all over the place.

MRS PIPER (*moving to him*) Whose were they?

BAXTER. I'll give you one guess.

(BAXTER *exits down* R. MRS PIPER *brushes the chair down* R. CLAIRE MARSHALL *knocks on the door up* C)

MRS PIPER. Come in.

(CLAIRE *enters up* C)

CLAIRE. Hello, Mrs Piper.

MRS PIPER. Oh, hello, dear!

CLAIRE. Has my husband gone home?

MRS PIPER. He's gone somewhere. He isn't here.

CLAIRE. That's strange. He asked me to call for him. (*She closes the door*)

MRS PIPER. The police are here!

CLAIRE (*moving down to the armchair*) Oh? Why?

MRS PIPER (*proudly*) I have produced new evidence.

CLAIRE. I don't understand. What is it?

MRS PIPER. I can't tell you that, madam. It's between me and the Big Five.

CLAIRE. I see.

MRS PIPER. I have to keep my own counsel.

CLAIRE. Oh, yes, of course! (*She sits in the armchair*)

MRS PIPER (R *of her*) I mean, I'd like to tell you. But it's a secret, really.

(CLAIRE *waits patiently*)

It's new evidence I deduced from my deductions after I read the *Evening Standard*. And found the button.

CLAIRE. Button?

MRS PIPER. But I can't talk about it. There was a bunch of keys, too, but we illuminated those. (*She turns back to the table*)

CLAIRE. Where are the police now?

MRS PIPER (*dusting the chair* R) Poking around somewhere.

CLAIRE. When my husband proved to be still alive I assumed that was the end of the affair. What else is there to solve?

MRS PIPER (*turning*) Ah! When I said it was Mr Marshall it must have been somebody else. Know what I think? I think——

(CLAIRE *looks in her handbag*)

it was somebody called Cameron.

CLAIRE (*looking up*) Cameron?

MRS PIPER. That's right. The button coincides with the ones on the waistcoat he was wearing. (*Crossing below the armchair to* LC) And I found it over here. Now then—(*she turns*) if he was murdered in a back alley in Notting Hill—why should I find his button in this office?

CLAIRE (*rising to* R *of her; alarmed*) Cameron? You said Cameron?

MRS PIPER. Oh, well, I can't talk about it. I'm the star witness. (*Moving to the fire exit to shake her duster*) It makes it a bit awkward.

(CLAIRE, *composing herself, turns to face up stage*)

(*Looking at her*) Are you feeling all right?

CLAIRE (*turning down stage*) It's so hot in here.

MRS PIPER (*moving to down* L *of the desk*) And it's the same blood group. I haven't to tell anyone about that, either.

CLAIRE (*taking off her coat and putting it over the back of the armchair*) Are you saying that someone called Cameron was murdered in this office? And his body has been found elsewhere?

D

MRS PIPER (*moving to* R *of the desk*) Ooh! I never said that! You'll get me shot.

CLAIRE (*moving to* R *of Mrs Piper*) Mrs Piper, you don't usually miss anything that goes on around here. You keep your eyes open . . .

MRS PIPER. That's my job.

(CLAIRE *hesitates, uncertain how to phrase her question*)

CLAIRE. On the evening when you thought you saw my husband's dead body . . .

MRS PIPER. Yes?

CLAIRE. A little earlier, perhaps—did you happen to see a man? I mean, did anyone ask you on which floor my husband's office is? Do you remember?

MRS PIPER. Wait a minute—yes, I do. He was reading the list of names—on the board in the vestibule. Tall and very handsome he was.

CLAIRE. Yes . . .

MRS PIPER. Lovely blue eyes and a moustache. He wore a grey suit the same as Mr Marshall. Who was he?

CLAIRE (*perturbed*) I don't know.

MRS PIPER. But you asked about him.

CLAIRE. No. What I meant was, if somebody was murdered here you might have seen *him* coming in. Do the police suspect anyone?

MRS PIPER. No, I don't think so. I'd know if they did. (*She turns to dust the desk*)

CLAIRE. Yes, I believe you would.

(BAXTER *enters down* R)

BAXTER (*surprised*) Oh! Mrs Marshall . . .

(MRS PIPER *returns to dusting the desk*)

CLAIRE (*moving* C) Good evening, Superintendent. I thought I'd catch my husband. I was too late.

BAXTER. I see. As you're here there's a question I'd like to ask you. (*He moves to* R *of the armchair*)

CLAIRE. Yes?

BAXTER. Have you ever heard of a man called James Cameron?

(MRS PIPER *reacts*)

CLAIRE (*with an effort*) I don't think so.

BAXTER. Try to remember.

CLAIRE. No, I don't think so. But, of course, one meets so many people. (*She sits in the armchair*)

BAXTER (*crossing above to* L *of her*) If you'd merely *met* him, Mrs Marshall, I'm not interested. Did you know him well?

CLAIRE. Unless my memory fails me—not at all. Why?

BAXTER. He's dead.

CLAIRE. Yes, so I understand.

(BAXTER *turns towards Mrs Piper*)

MRS PIPER (*moving to* L *of Baxter*) It slipped out.
BAXTER. I'll bet it did! What else have you been saying?
MRS PIPER. Nothing. You know me—"Old Sealed Lips".
BAXTER. When I wish the public to be informed of my activities I shall announce it through the regular channels of radio, television and the national press. Not through Mrs Piper.
MRS PIPER. Oo, he does shout!
BAXTER (*to Claire*) Was James Cameron your lover?

(MRS PIPER *returns to dusting* L *of the desk*)

CLAIRE (*rising, leaving her bag in the armchair*) That's a ridiculous question.
BAXTER. You've already admitted such a person exists. Do you still refuse to tell me his name?
CLAIRE (*moving up* C) It doesn't concern you.
BAXTER (*following her*) If he's been murdered everything *concerning* him concerns me. You insist you didn't know James Cameron?
CLAIRE. I do.

(*The telephone on the desk rings*)

MRS PIPER (*picking up the receiver*) Hello, yes, who is it? . . . Oh, how are you?
BAXTER. Who is it?
MRS PIPER. Ssh! (*Into the phone*) How are things goin', then? . . . Oh, I say—fancy that!
BAXTER (*moving towards her*) Who is it?
MRS PIPER. Inspector Willis. (*She returns to the phone*)
BAXTER (*roaring*) Give me that phone!!

(*They both wrestle with it and finally* BAXTER *pulls it away*)

(*Into the phone*) Willis? Baxter . . . Yes? Description of the man? (*He pulls the jotter pad and pen towards him and writes*)

(CLAIRE *moves to the armchair*)

Go ahead! . . . Wore a grey suit . . . Red tie . . . Dark hair . . . Age about forty . . .
MRS PIPER (*to Claire*) It's him! That's the one. (*She crosses above Baxter to* R *of him*)

(CLAIRE *sits on the* L *arm of the armchair*)

BAXTER. Will you be quiet! (*Into the phone*) Yes?
MRS PIPER. Moustache.
BAXTER (*into the phone*) Moustache.
MRS PIPER. Blue eyes.
BAXTER. Blue eyes.
MRS PIPER. Six feet in his socks.

BAXTER. About six feet tall . . . (*He stops; he stares at her*) Right! (*He replaces the receiver and, puzzled, moves to* L *of Mrs Piper*) Let's have it! Do you know him, were you guessing, or are you psychic?

MRS PIPER. 'E was 'ere the night of the murder.

BAXTER. Was he now? Why didn't you say so?

MRS PIPER. Didn't seem worthwhile. You said it was one of us.

BAXTER. Did this man speak to you?

MRS PIPER. Yes. He asked which floor Marshall Developments was on. I said it was on the top floor but I thought everybody'd gone home.

BAXTER. What time was that?

MRS PIPER. About eight o'clock.

BAXTER. By your clock or by Big Ben?

MRS PIPER. Oh, give over! (*She picks up her duster and brush from the desk*) He is a tease.

BAXTER (*following her*) When you told this man the offices were empty what did he say?

MRS PIPER (*moving down* R) I beg your pardon, dear?

BAXTER (*moving to* R *of her*) When you told him the offices were empty, what did he say?

MRS PIPER. "Thank you."

BAXTER (*impatiently*) And after he'd said "Thank you"?

MRS PIPER. "Good night."

BAXTER. And after that?

MRS PIPER. He went to the lift and got in it.

BAXTER. In other words, he ignored the fact that no-one was likely to be in. He got in the lift and came up to this floor?

MRS PIPER. He got in. I didn't see where he got out.

BAXTER. And you didn't see him come back again?

MRS PIPER (*shaking her head*) No, darling. (*She puts the brush and duster in the bucket*)

BAXTER (*moving to up* R *of Claire*) Mr Marshall *was* still here. According to Miss Selby he had an appointment with a Mr Warfield at eight-fifteen. And around that time a man arrived whose description fits that of James Cameron. Which is just about the time medical evidence states that he died. I think I ought to have another chat with your husband, Mrs Marshall. I'd like to know more about Mr Warfield. (*Crossing above to* L *of Claire*) I'd like to know if he arrived. If he did your husband would have an alibi, wouldn't he?

CLAIRE. Yes—(*facing him*) I suppose he would.

BAXTER. In view of this, Mrs Marshall, you'd be wise to answer my earlier question. Did you know James Cameron?

CLAIRE (*turning away*) Yes.

BAXTER. Was he your—friend?

CLAIRE. Yes.

BAXTER. The man you were meeting secretly?

CLAIRE. I told you. Yes!

BAXTER. Thank you. (*He moves away* LC) Now we can start again.

CLAIRE. That's all I can tell you.
BAXTER. I hope not.
CLAIRE. I didn't know of his death. I hadn't the faintest idea.
You don't suspect me, do you?
MRS PIPER (R *of the armchair*) No, no, of course he doesn't, dear. He
suspects your husband.

(BAXTER *turns to Mrs Piper.* GODDARD *enters up* C *and stands* R *of
the door*)

GODDARD. Mr Marshall, sir.

(MARSHALL *enters and moves to* C, *above the armchair.* GODDARD
exits, closing the door)

MARSHALL. You wanted to see me. What is it this time? Another
body?
BAXTER (L *of him*) That's right, Mr Marshall. Another body.
MARSHALL (*surprised*) What?
BAXTER. Found in a back alley in Notting Hill.
MARSHALL. Oh—well—what has that got to do with us?
BAXTER. His name was James Cameron. Have you ever heard of
him, sir?
MARSHALL. No, I don't think so.
BAXTER. You're sure?
MRS PIPER. He means you *ought* to have heard of him, because . . .
BAXTER. Please, Mrs Piper!

(MRS PIPER *moves down* R)

(*To Marshall*) He was a friend of your wife's, sir.
CLAIRE (*rising*) You suspected there was someone, didn't you?
You were wrong, thinking it was Robert Westerby. It was James
Cameron. If only you'd been kinder, given me more of your time . . .
(*She begins to cry and sits again*)

(MARSHALL *puts his hat on the desk*)

MRS PIPER. I'll go and get us all a nice cup of tea. How's that?
(*She moves up* C)

(CLAIRE *smiles*)

BAXTER (*crossing below Marshall to above the armchair*) That's the
best idea you've had yet.
MRS PIPER. Don't worry, if we wait long enough you might have
one too.

(MRS PIPER *exits up* C, *closing the door*)

BAXTER. Cameron is dead, Mr Marshall. Did you know that?
MARSHALL. How could I?
BAXTER. On the night he was murdered you stayed late at your
office.

MARSHALL (*moving down* L) So did thousands of business men.

BAXTER (*moving to* C) Yes, sir, but he didn't visit their offices, and he did visit yours.

MARSHALL. You mean he came here? To see me?

BAXTER. I don't know. Did he?

MARSHALL. Certainly not! I never met the man in my life. (*Earnestly*) I'm telling the truth. We never spoke to each other.

BAXTER. You had an appointment for eight-fifteen with a Mr Warfield.

MARSHALL. Yes.

BAXTER. Did you keep that appointment?

MARSHALL. Yes. No, that's misleading. I did. He didn't.

BAXTER. Mr Warfield didn't turn up?

MARSHALL. No.

BAXTER. Do you know why he didn't?

MARSHALL. I've no idea, and no way of finding out. He wrote to me—a personal letter addressed to my house—arranging to meet me that evening.

BAXTER. Here in your office?

MARSHALL. No. There's a café round the corner. He said he'd be there.

BAXTER. How were you to recognize him?

MARSHALL. He said he'd approach me.

BAXTER. I suppose you have his address?

MARSHALL. There was no address on the notepaper.

(BAXTER *turns away*)

You don't believe me? All right.

(*He takes a note from his pocket and hands it to* BAXTER, *who reads it*)

No, don't keep it to yourself—let's have it out loud. My wife and I have no secrets from each other. Have we, darling?

(CLAIRE *turns away*)

I'm sorry. Warfield claimed to know the name of your boy friend. He promised to tell me. Presumably when we met he intended to ask for money. But he didn't arrive. (*To Baxter*) And that's the truth.

BAXTER. It's typewritten.

MARSHALL. So that it can't be traced.

BAXTER. Can't it, sir? (*He crosses above the armchair to the table down* R, *sits, uncovers the typewriter, inserts a sheet of paper and types*)

(MARSHALL *steps in to* C, *exchanging a look with Claire.* MRS PIPER *enters up* C)

MRS PIPER. Have I missed anything? (*She closes the door and moves to above the armchair*) The kettle's on, dear. (*Crossing to up stage of the table* R) What are you doing—writing your memoirs?

(BAXTER *pulls the paper from the typewriter and rises*)

BAXTER. Just as I thought. (*He crosses below Mrs Piper to* R *of Marshall*)

(MRS PIPER *moves in to* R *of Baxter*)

This letter was typed on an identical machine to this.

MARSHALL. Are you suggesting one of my employees is responsible?

BAXTER. Either that—or their employer.

MRS PIPER (*raises a hand*) Excuse me, may I ask Mr Marshall a question?

BAXTER. No.

(MRS PIPER *taps him on the shoulder and as he turns, dodges round behind him to* R *of Marshall*)

MRS PIPER. Are you sure you never heard of Mr Cameron, sir?

(BAXTER *moves* R *to below the table, folding the paper*)

MARSHALL. Yes.

MRS PIPER. Because when you and I were alone in here earlier on you was sat doodling at your desk. And afterwards when I come to empty the ashtray I glanced at the pad and you'd written J.C. all over it.

(BAXTER *turns*)

Well, I mean, J.C. could stand for James Cameron, couldn't it?

MARSHALL. You're mistaken.

MRS PIPER. I don't think I am, sir. 'Cos I kept the paper. (*Moving to* L *of Baxter*) I've changed me hiding-place. (*She fishes down her dress front*) If I can ever find anything but crumbs down here. (*Producing the paper*) 'Ere we are. (*She hands it to Baxter*) Hot evidence.

(MRS PIPER *exits up* C)

BAXTER. Well, sir?

MARSHALL. All right. I admit I knew about him. But not until last night. Warfield, whoever he is, didn't turn up, so I came back here to my office expecting an overseas phone call. When I arrived there was a note waiting for me on my desk. It said, "The man's name is James Cameron."

BAXTER (*disbelievingly*) May I see this message?

MARSHALL. I destroyed it. But it wouldn't prove anything, would it? I could have typed it myself. Do you think I murdered him?

BAXTER. My enquiries have only just started. (*He pockets the paper and moves up* R)

MARSHALL (*following to up* C) Now look here, Superintendent . . .
CLAIRE (*rising, to* L *of Marshall*) Richard! Don't!

(BAXTER *puts on his coat*)

MARSHALL. It's coincidence, that's all. I can give honest answers to every question. I didn't kill him. I never saw him *alive* . . . (*He hesitates*)

(*They stare at him*)

BAXTER. Never saw him *alive?*

(MRS PIPER *enters up* C)

MRS PIPER. 'Ere we are, dears. Tea up!

(GODDARD *enters with the tray. Suddenly* MARSHALL *rushes between them, and in the confusion escapes, locking the door from the outside.*
  As MARSHALL *exits, he pushes Goddard down on to Baxter's lap on the chair up* R. MRS PIPER *takes the tray and crosses to put it on the* R *end of the desk.* BAXTER *pushes Goddard up*)

BAXTER. Goddard, you blithering idiot, get after him!
GODDARD (*trying the door handle*) He's locked it, sir.
BAXTER. Put your shoulder to it, man.
GODDARD. Yes, sir. (*Rather ineffectually, he shoulders the door*)
BAXTER. Oh, get out of the way.

(GODDARD *moves to* L *of the door.* BAXTER *backs away and runs to the door.* MRS PIPER *runs to stop him*)

MRS PIPER. 'Arry, you'll do yourself a mischief. What's the matter with that door? (*She points to the door* R *and crosses back to the desk*)
BAXTER. Bring him back, Goddard.
GODDARD. Yes, sir.

(GODDARD *exits down* R)

BAXTER. He won't get far.
CLAIRE (*moving to* L *of Baxter*) Are you sure he's responsible? Aren't you, perhaps, making a mistake?

(MRS PIPER *pours tea*)

BAXTER. If he hasn't got a guilty conscience, why did he run away?
CLAIRE. I simply don't know. (*She picks up her bag and coat*) May I go now, please?
MRS PIPER. 'Ere, don't you want your tea? (*She moves to* C, *holding a cup*)
CLAIRE. I'm sorry, Mrs Piper. I . . . (*To Baxter*) You don't want me to stay, do you?
BAXTER. No, go home, Mrs Marshall. I'll phone you later if I have any news.

(CLAIRE *exits down* R, *closing the door*)

MRS PIPER (*moving back to the desk to put sugar in the tea*) Oh, well—
I'm going to 'ave it then. I can drink tea till it comes out of me ears.
'Ow about you, 'Arry?

BAXTER. No, thanks. (*Checking notes*) We don't seem able to hold
on to anything around here, do we? Dead bodies move. Buttons
are stolen. Living people vanish in front of our eyes.

MRS PIPER (*moving up* R) It's as if the place was haunted. (*She drinks
the tea*)

BAXTER (*crossing below her to above the desk*) If it is I know who
haunts it. Oh, the paper-knife! You said you thought that was the
murder weapon, didn't you? I'd better take it. I don't suppose
there'll be anything on it, but . . . (*He is searching the desk*) Where is
it?

MRS PIPER. On Mr Marshall's desk.

BAXTER. No, it isn't.

MRS PIPER. It ought to be.

BAXTER. I *know* it ought to be.

MRS PIPER. But it isn't. (*She steps towards the desk and puts down her
cup*)

BAXTER. I know it isn't.

MRS PIPER. Well, perhaps it's under the blotto.

BAXTER (*lifting the blotter*) No, it *isn't* under the blotto.

MRS PIPER. All right, then! It's been here all the time.

BAXTER. Why isn't it here now? (*He moves below the desk*)

MRS PIPER. 'Cos it's *gone*.

(BAXTER *throws his hat angrily on the floor down* C)

BAXTER. If you say that word again . . .

MRS PIPER (*coming below the desk to* R *of him*) Well, it 'as gone, 'asn't
it?

BAXTER. Everything disappears round here. What are you, a
conjuror? (*He bends down to pick up his hat*)

MRS PIPER. If I was, you'd 'ave disappeared for a start.

BAXTER. What did you say?

MRS PIPER. Oh, get lost!

BAXTER, *in a fury, jams his hat on her head, crosses below her to the
door up* C, *and finds it locked.*

CURTAIN

ACT III

SCENE—*The same. About four-thirty the following afternoon.*

It is dull, and the sky is stormy. The lights, therefore, are on.

When the CURTAIN *rises,* MARIAN SELBY *is sitting at the table down* R *but, obviously uneasy, is not working.* VICKIE REYNOLDS *looks in up* C, *then enters, holding a cup of tea.*

VICKIE. What are we supposed to do? I've been sitting in there all day doing nothing.

MARIAN (*rising, with some papers in her hand*) Is that unusual?

VICKIE. No—but it's no fun doing nothing, if you haven't been given something to do.

(MARIAN *crosses below the armchair to* L *of the desk and round to above it*)

Miss Selby, you shouldn't be mean to me about Mr Marshall. (*She moves to above the* R *end of the desk*) It wasn't my fault he made a pass at me

MARIAN. He was only being friendly. (*She opens the blotter*)

VICKIE. Middle-aged men are like that, aren't they? The older— the flipping friendlier.

(MARIAN *snaps the blotter shut*)

Isn't it funny how sex gets hold of you?

(MARIAN *glances away*)

(*Awkwardly*) You know what I mean. No, perhaps not.

(MARIAN *moves below the desk to her table down* R)

(*More brightly*) I say, *you* don't think the boss is a murderer, do you?

MARIAN. I know he isn't. But, as long as he hides, a number of stupid people are sure to think he is.

VICKIE. Do you think he should give himself up?

MARIAN (*sitting at her table*) I'd rather not discuss it, if you don't mind.

VICKIE. Oh, all right! Only, with no work to do, I don't know how I'm going to pass the time. (*She begins to yawn*)

MARIAN. What do you usually do?

(VICKIE *stops yawning and looks exasperated.* ROBERT WESTERBY *enters down* R *with a file of papers*)

VICKIE. Any news, Mr Westerby?

ROBERT (*putting a paper on the table above Marian and crossing to down* L) Hasn't Miss Selby told you? Mr Logan came back from his holiday last Thursday.

VICKIE. No!

MARIAN. There are floods in Brittany. He thought he'd be better off at home.

VICKIE. Oh! Do you think *he* did it?

ROBERT. Of course not, but at the time of the murder he *was* in London. So he's got to be considered now along with everybody else.

(MRS PIPER *and* BAXTER *enter up* C. MRS PIPER *is clinging to his* L *arm and holding a brandy flask.* GODDARD *follows them, then takes off his coat, puts it on the chair* R *of the outer door and remains in the anteroom.* BAXTER *leads Mrs Piper to the chair* R *of the desk.* VICKIE *moves to above the chair*)

BAXTER. You'd better sit down.

(MRS PIPER *sits*)

VICKIE. Are you all right?

MRS PIPER. I still feel a bit faintified.

VICKIE. Can I get you a cup of tea?

BAXTER. Tea! She's had the best part of a flask of brandy already. (*He tries to take the flask*)

MRS PIPER (*holding on to the flask*) Still, I better hang on to it, eh! In case I come over queer again.

VICKIE. I'm in there if they want me. (*She goes to the passage and stands* R *of Goddard, talking*)

ROBERT. Is she ill?

BAXTER. Mrs Piper has been with me on a rather unpleasant mission. To identify the body of James Cameron.

ROBERT. Oh, I see. I'm sorry.

MRS PIPER. It was him all right.

MARIAN. I didn't know she knew him.

BAXTER. She confirms he is the man who came to this building the night he was murdered. He spoke to her. Excuse me a moment. Goddard!

(BAXTER *goes into the passage to talk to Goddard.* VICKIE *exits off up* R. ROBERT *moves to* L *of the desk with papers*)

MRS PIPER (*drinking*) 'E was a 'andsome man. If it 'adn't been for the scar across 'is face 'e'd 'ave been *very* 'andsome.

ROBERT. Scar on his face? (*He leaves papers in the blotter and closes it*)

MRS PIPER. Like those Persian officers at Idleberg in the *Student Prince.* (*Indicating her cheek*) Across 'ere.

(ROBERT *leaves the file on the up* R *end of the desk*)

(*To Baxter*) You can have that back now, 'Arry. I feel a king to what I was.

(BAXTER *comes back into the room, takes the flask, shakes and upturns it*)

There, now, it must have evaporated.

(BAXTER *grabs the top, closes the flask and puts it in his pocket*)

MARIAN. Is there no news of Mr Marshall?

(ROBERT *moves down* L)

BAXTER. Not yet. But it's merely a matter of time.
MARIAN. Do *you* think he's the murderer?
BAXTER. I'm not here to answer questions, Miss Selby. (*He takes off his hat and coat, crosses above, and puts them on the desk chair*)

(*There is an uncomfortable silence*)

MRS PIPER. No. Mr Marshall didn't do it.
BAXTER (*turning to her*) Didn't he?
MRS PIPER. No.
BAXTER. Oh! I suppose you know who did?
MRS PIPER. I might.

(BAXTER *faces her, hands on hips*)

BAXTER. We'd better go into consultation.
MRS PIPER. You could do with a second opinion.

(GODDARD *enters up* C *holding the door open*)

GODDARD. Mrs Marshall, sir.

(CLAIRE *enters*, R *of Goddard*)

BAXTER (*moving to* L *of her*) Oh, Mrs Marshall, thank you for coming.
CLAIRE. Have you any news of my husband?
BAXTER. I'm afraid not. Won't you sit down?
CLAIRE. Thank you. Hello, Robert. (*She sits in the armchair*)
BAXTER (*to Goddard*) Ask Miss Reynolds to come in, will you?
GODDARD (*calling off*) Will you come in, please, Miss Reynolds?

(ROBERT *sits down* L. VICKIE *enters up* C)

VICKIE (*to Goddard*) Did you want me?

(GODDARD *exits, closing the door*)

BAXTER. Yes, I want to speak to all of you. There's a chair there, Miss Reynolds.

(VICKIE *sits up* R)

Now, ladies and gentlemen, this case is unique in my experience . . .

MRS PIPER. And mine.

BAXTER (*moving down* L, *then across to down* R, *then above the armchair to* C) First the body disappears—dead—and then it comes back—alive. Then the button disappears. Then the murder weapon. Now Marshall has disappeared. For the second time! Finally, Mr Logan, in whose office the corpse was first seen, turns out to have been in London all the time. Why did no-one tell me?

ROBERT. We didn't know. At least, I didn't.

MARIAN. Nor did I until last evening.

VICKIE. I've only just heard about it.

MRS PIPER (*quietly*) I knew.

BAXTER (*turning*) It would have been a friendly gesture if you had taken me into your confidence.

MRS PIPER. You told me only to say Yes and No.

BAXTER. It is your duty—(*to the others also*) *everybody's* duty—to give me all relevant information.

MRS PIPER. Every time I open my mouth you tell me to shut it.

BAXTER. Because it's open when it should be shut, and shut when it should be open.

MRS PIPER. Anyway, he didn't murder anyone. Not Mr Logan.

BAXTER. What I should have made of this enquiry without your help I tremble to think.

MRS PIPER. No. Doesn't bear thinking about, do it?

BAXTER. How did you know he was in London?

MRS PIPER. He rung me up to ask if I knew where his fountain pen was.

BAXTER. You should have told me.

MRS PIPER. Why? Did *you* know where it was?

BAXTER (*moving above the armchair; to Marian*) Miss Selby, you knew he was in London. He telephoned you last night.

MARIAN. I didn't think it was important.

BAXTER (*moving to* R; *to Robert*) And you, Mr Westerby?

ROBERT. Miss Selby told me. But not until this morning. If Mr Marshall was dead we were all under suspicion. But now—as far as I can see—Logan is no more involved than—well, than you are.

(MRS PIPER *laughs.* BAXTER *reacts, then moves to* R *of Robert*)

BAXTER. Mr Logan is very deeply involved. He telephoned me at nine o'clock last night. I arranged to visit him at his flat. I got there at nine-forty. Mr Logan was dead.

MARIAN. He was—what?

BAXTER (*turning*) Murdered, Miss Selby.

MRS PIPER (*rising to up* C) 'Ere, I'm getting out of here.

VICKIE (*rising to* R *of Mrs Piper, leading her back to sit as before, and standing behind her*) It's all right, love. You'll be safe here. Sit down.

ROBERT. You can't be serious.

BAXTER. Mr Westerby, that's just one thing I *can* be. Mr Logan

had some information which he implied might be useful to me.
Someone got to him before I did, and murdered him.
   VICKIE. Do you know who?
   BAXTER. No, Miss Reynolds. Do you?
   VICKIE. Who, me? Why *me?*
   BAXTER. A woman was seen to arrive at his flat at ten minutes
past nine. Was it you?
   MRS PIPER. She wouldn't kill any man. She's too fond of them
to go cutting short the supply

   (VICKIE *moves above the desk to sit on the* R *arm of the desk chair*)

   BAXTER (*moving to* L *of Claire*) Mrs Marshall?
   CLAIRE. I don't even know where he lives.
   BAXTER (*crossing to Marian*) Miss Selby?
   MARIAN. Are you asking me if I killed Mr Logan?
   BAXTER. I'm asking you if you called to see him at his flat in
Surbiton last night.
   MARIAN. No.
   MRS PIPER. I did.

   (BAXTER *crosses to* R *of Mrs Piper*)

   BAXTER. Are you telling me you went to see Logan at his flat?
   MRS PIPER (*nodding*) Yes.
   BAXTER. Last night?
   MRS PIPER (*nodding*) Yes.
   BAXTER. May I ask why?
   MRS PIPER. To fetch him his fountain pen.
   BAXTER. Is that the only reason?
   MRS PIPER. No.
   BAXTER (*fiercely*) What other reason?
   MRS PIPER. I don't like the way you're conducting this case.
Well, I don't. Mr Marshall's got himself involved, and you're in-
volving him worser. I went to ask if Mr Logan could throw any
light on the proceedings
   BAXTER. I have half a mind to arrest you and throw you into jail.
Of all the interfering, bothersome busybodies . . .
   MRS PIPER. I know my rights. (*Rising*) I can visit my colleagues
on the staff any time I want to. And you can't stop me.
   BAXTER. Did you murder him whilst you were there?
   MRS PIPER. Oh! Just ignore him. (*She crosses below Baxter to above
the armchair*)
   BAXTER. Was he alive when you got there?
   MRS PIPER. Yes. *And* when I left.
   BAXTER (*moving to* L *of her*) What time was that?
   MRS PIPER. Before nine o'clock.
   BAXTER. What did you talk about?
   MRS PIPER. His fountain pen.
   BAXTER. And then you came straight back here?

Mrs Piper. I called in for a couple on my way back. Crumbs, 'ave a heart!

Baxter. Did Mr Logan say anything to you about the information he was going to give me?

(Mrs Piper *hesitates uncomfortably, glancing at the others*)

Mrs Piper. Not exactly.

Baxter. Did he? Yes or no?

Mrs Piper. No.

Baxter. You hesitated. Why?

Mrs Piper. Because you're so snappy. You get me flummoxed. (*She sits up* R)

(Baxter, *his hands behind his back, paces thoughtfully*)

Baxter (*crossing to* c) So, we now have two murders on our hands. What I ask myself is, was Mr Marshall aware—(*moving to the chair* R *of the desk*) that Logan was in London? Could he have known he intended to contact me? Who sneaked into Logan's flat last night? And who, to save his skin, removed the witness by stabbing him in the back? (*Dramatically*) Who?

Mrs Piper. If you want my opinion . . .

Baxter. I do not want your opinion. I am putting before you a hypothetical question which does not call for an answer.

Mrs Piper. Oh! I see. (*To Marian*) What's hypothetical?

Baxter. Who—(*moving down* LC) I ask again—was the young and beautiful woman who was observed to call on Logan last night? (*He pauses for effect*)

Mrs Piper (*very seriously*) I told you. *Me*.

Claire (*rising and moving* c) Superintendent, you think my husband murdered James Cameron. Do you also think he killed Mr Logan? Oh, yes, I know you're not here to answer questions, but the circumstances are exceptional.

Baxter. All right. I will tell you what I think happened. (*He crosses above the armchair*) I shall do so hoping that one or other of you will recall some point which agrees with what I say.

(Claire *sits on the chair* R *of the desk*)

Mrs Piper. Or disagrees!

Baxter (*swallowing hard*) Or disagrees. Now, then. (*He faces them dramatically*) We know that Richard Marshall knew of your—(*facing* Claire) infidelity. Suppose he'd found out it was James Cameron And suppose he made arrangements to see him here—when no-one was likely to be about. They met. They quarrelled, and in a rage, he killed him. What must he do next? Get rid of the body. His car was already parked at the back of the building. He obviously couldn't take the body down the front stairs without being seen. The only alternative was to use the service stairs which he could reach through this office and across the flat roof. Unfortunately for him someone entered Logan's office—the deputy caretaker.

MRS PIPER. Oh, chase me!

BAXTER. He heard her coming and hid.

MRS PIPER. Where?

BAXTER. Well, behind the curtains.

MRS PIPER. There aren't any curtains in Mr Logan's office.

BAXTER (*struggling for an idea*) Behind the desk.

MRS PIPER. It's only a table. You can see through it.

BAXTER. In the cupboard.

MRS PIPER. There isn't one.

BAXTER (*shouting*) Behind the blasted door then! And please don't interrupt when I'm speaking. Now where was I?

MRS PIPER. Behind the blasted door.

BAXTER. Whilst Marshall was hiding Mrs Piper entered the office —and saw the dead body. When she ran out of the room in a panic, your husband dragged the body in here. Later he used the service stairs, drove off and left the body where it was eventually found. Does that sound reasonable?

CLAIRE. You forget one thing. She didn't see Mr Cameron in here. She said she saw my husband.

BAXTER. She couldn't have done. He wasn't dead, was he? Mrs Piper came back quicker than he'd expected, and she came in here. He had to think quickly, so what did he do?

MRS PIPER. Are you asking me?

BAXTER (*moving above the desk to between Claire and Vickie*) Suppose he'd already put Cameron's body in the car and had come back for something, the murder weapon perhaps, or to make sure he'd left no evidence. He heard Mrs Piper coming, flung himself into that chair and pretended to be the body. After she'd gone he completed his work—(*crossing to R of Claire*) and made his escape, turning up later to discredit her story. Does that satisfy you, Mrs Marshall?

MRS PIPER. It doesn't satisfy me.

BAXTER. We must satisfy *you* at all costs. If I have misunderstood your evidence I am prepared to be told where, when and how.

MRS PIPER. It wasn't like that at all.

BAXTER. Did you or did you not go into Logan's office and see the apparently dead body of a man?

MRS PIPER. Yes, I did.

BAXTER. Did you then come in here and see the apparently dead body of Richard Marshall?

MRS PIPER. Yes, but . . .

BAXTER. Thank you, Mrs Piper. (*To Claire*) But your husband was not dead, Mrs Marshall. And, confronted by these facts, he chose to run away. Why?

MRS PIPER. That isn't what happened at all.

BAXTER. Be quiet!

MRS PIPER (*rising to R of Baxter; determinedly*) I won't be quiet.

You can arrest me if you want to, but I won't sit like a dummy and watch you convict an innocent man. Let me tell you what happened.

BAXTER. No. (*He turns away from her*)

ROBERT. I think you should, Superintendent. After all, she's your star witness.

BAXTER. Star witness!

CLAIRE. Hear what she has to say. Please!

BAXTER. It's out of the question.

(CLAIRE *takes a cigarette from her bag.* ROBERT *moves below the desk and lights it for her*)

MRS PIPER (*to Baxter*) Ooh! You always was stubborn, 'Arry Baxter, but now you're pig-headed.

BAXTER. Oh, well, I'm due to retire fairly soon. Describe to us, Mrs Piper, the case as you see it. (*He blows his nose*)

MRS PIPER (*unabashed*) Well, it's like this . . .

BAXTER. Just a minute—are we about to learn what happened, or what you *think* happened?

MRS PIPER. A bit of both. Now the boss—(*turning to face Claire and Robert*) thought there was something going on between you two and he didn't believe Mr Westerby when he denied it. Then on this Thursday evening this 'ere Warfield was supposed to call and see the boss. Well, he didn't turn up—(*turning to Baxter*) but he sent a note saying, "The name you want is James Cameron."

(ROBERT *sits down* R)

BAXTER. Yes, we know all that.

MRS PIPER. I know we know all that. But what you don't know is what else was on the note. It went on to say, "He is—(*she moves above the armchair*) in Logan's office now."

BAXTER. How do you know all this?

MRS PIPER. Who's interrupting now? Stop it! It's not ethical. (*Moving to* C) 'Course, the boss couldn't make heads or tails of it so he went to investigate and there in Mr Logan's office was a dead body. Well, he was in a hell of a fix but he couldn't get out because the murderer had locked the door.

BAXTER. How do you know all this?

MRS PIPER. I'm just submerging, ain't I? But he must have been in a terrible fix when I came along and unlocked it. There was nothing left for him to do but hide behind it. As soon as I saw the dead body I ran straight down to tell Fred and *then*, 'Arry, *then* he did everything like you said he did. (*Stepping up stage and pointing off*) In Mr Logan's office. (*Stepping* C) In here across the flat roof—(*moving* LC) and down the service stairs. He knew he'd been framed and he says he's speaking the truth and I believe him.

(ROBERT, CLAIRE and VICKIE *all rise and group round Mrs Piper, speaking together*)

E

ROBERT ⎤   ⎡ Well done, Mrs Piper!
VICKIE ⎥ (together)   ⎨ Aren't you clever, love!
CLAIRE ⎦   ⎣ Mrs Piper, I'm so grateful.
MRS PIPER. Well, it's just my conjecture, of course.
ROBERT. And a very good one, too.
    CLAIRE (passing Mrs Piper across her to the armchair) Come and sit
down, Mrs Piper.

    (MRS PIPER sits in the armchair. CLAIRE stands L of her, and ROBERT
L of Claire. VICKIE moves above the armchair)

VICKIE. Fancy you working all that out!

    (There is a general ad lib. talk until BAXTER cuts in)

    BAXTER. Just a minute! Just a minute! You never conjectured
as much as that in all your life. (He moves up to the door and opens it)
Goddard! (To Mrs Piper) If what I'm thinking is true, Lily Piper,
I'll put you away for ten years.
MRS PIPER. I don't know what you're gassing about.
BAXTER. Marshall. That's what I'm gassing about.

    (GODDARD enters up C. ROBERT moves away L)

GODDARD. Yes, sir.
    BAXTER. Go down to the basement to Mrs Piper's flat. You'll
find Richard Marshall there. Bring him up here double quick.
GODDARD. I didn't know he was there, sir.
BAXTER. Mrs Busybody did. Go on, man, move.
GODDARD. Yes, sir.

    (GODDARD exits up C, leaving the inner door open and closing the outer
door after him)

    BAXTER (moving to R of Mrs Piper) All right. I'm all ears. How did
you hide him?

    (VICKIE moves slowly across above to close the door and then sits in the
chair up R)

    MRS PIPER. Oh, well, I might as well tell you the rest of it now.
When he ran out of here last night, Mr Marshall went straight down
to mine in the basement. Fred let him in and when I got there I
was flabbergasted—there was the both of them having a smoke and
a cup of tea in my kitchen, and he told me everything just as I told
you. And I knew he was speaking the truth. That's why I said I'd
try and help him. I never liked him much, but I do now. (Rising)
'Arry, he's not a bad man, he hasn't killed anybody.
    BAXTER. In other words, when Logan telephoned you, Mr
Marshall knew about it?
    MRS PIPER. Yes, but he couldn't harm him, could he? He never
left here.
    BAXTER. Did he ask you to visit Logan at his flat?

Mrs Piper. No.

Baxter (*crossing below her to* lc) Where was he whilst you were out?

Mrs Piper. In my kitchen.

Baxter. Where was your husband?

Mrs Piper. Where do you think he was after opening time?

Baxter (*turning and pouncing*) Then Marshall hasn't got an alibi! He could have gone out.

Mrs Piper. He could have, but he didn't.

(Baxter *crosses below* r *of the armchair to above it*)

Baxter. Now you're conjecturing again.

Mrs Piper. Oo, you are hard to convince!

Baxter (*above the armchair*) I stick to facts and demand proof. Marshall has no alibi to prove he wasn't responsible for Logan's death.

Mrs Piper (*moving to* l *of Baxter*) 'E doesn't 'ave to prove 'e didn't. You 'ave to prove 'e did. (*To the others*) I know the law. (*To Baxter*) And you can't prove 'e did, 'cos I know 'e didn't. So there! (*She sits* r *of the desk*)

(Goddard *enters up* c, *to* r *of the doorway*)

Goddard. Mr Marshall, sir.

(Marshall *enters up* c, l *of Goddard and moves to* c. Goddard *closes the door and stands* r *of it*)

Baxter. Welcome back, Mr Marshall.

Claire. Richard! (*Moving up to* l *of him*) Thank God you're all right.

Marshall. I suppose it was stupid of me.

Baxter (r *of Marshall*) It was, sir.

Marshall. I hope Mrs Piper won't suffer for it. She's been very kind.

Mrs Piper. Oh, that's quite a pleasure, sir.

Baxter (*moving to* r *of Mrs Piper*) She knows the law. She just told us so. (*To Mrs Piper*) What is the penalty for assisting a suspected criminal to escape?

Mrs Piper. He can't wait to see me in goal.

Marshall. Am I under arrest?

Baxter. I shall have to ask you to accompany me to the station for further questioning. You're not under arrest—yet.

Claire. Richard, please forgive me. It's all my fault.

Marshall. No, I'm to blame as much as you are. I'm sorry.

(Goddard *opens the door and stands against it holding the handle*)

Shall we go? (*He moves to the door up* c)

Baxter. First of all we'll take another look in Logan's office.

I'd like you to show me what you claim happened. (*To Mrs Piper*)
You'd better come along too.

Mrs Piper (*rising*) Well, I'll come if you want me to, dear, but
I don't want to interfere.

(Mrs Piper *exits up* c. Claire *follows her and waits in the doorway.*
Baxter *moves to* l *of the doorway.* Marshall *goes up to the door and
turns*)

Marshall (*to Vickie and Marian*) There's no point in the rest of
you staying. You might as well go home.

Vickie (*delighted*) Oh, thank you!

Marian (*rising; eagerly*) But surely there is something I can
do . . . ?

Marshall. No. Take the rest of the day off.

Marian. Oh, but, Mr Marshall . . .

(*After* Marshall *turns away* Marian *covers the typewriter, picks up
her handbag and pushes the chair in to the desk*)

Marshall. No. (*To Robert*) Westerby, you might put a call
through to Birmingham before you go. Tell them I can't possibly
see them tomorrow.

Robert. Yes, of course.

Marshall. Oh, and Jacques Frères in Paris. We've a meeting
later in the week. Postpone it.

Robert. I'll make an excuse.

Marshall. Thank you. (*He turns to the door*)

Vickie (*rising; tactlessly*) Will you be here tomorrow, Mr Marshall?
Oh, sorry! (*She sits*)

(Marshall *does not reply.* Claire *goes weepily to him. He puts his
arm round her.* Claire *and* Marshall *exit up* c, *followed by* Baxter.
Goddard *remains by the door,* l *of Vickie*)

Marian (*to Robert*) I feel so helpless. (*She moves up* c, *puts her bag
on the chair* r *of the desk, and takes her coat from the cupboard*)

Robert (*l of the desk*) Yes, I know.

Marian (*to Goddard*) He thinks Mr Marshall is guilty, doesn't he?
(*She puts her coat on the chair* r *of the desk and closes the cupboard*)

Goddard. No comment, madam.

(Robert *crosses to up* c. Marian *moves above the desk to the window*)

Robert. I say, I wonder who the young and attractive woman
was who called on Logan last night.

Vickie. He had girls friends, didn't he? Anyway, it was a man
who killed him.

Robert. Who says so?

Vickie. A woman couldn't have done it. She wouldn't be strong
enough.

Robert. That isn't true. Take Miss Selby, for example—she's

almost as tall as I am. Pretty strong, too. Lots of women are. (*To Goddard*) Don't you agree?

GODDARD. No comment, sir.

MARIAN (*at the window*) It looks like a storm.

(MARIAN *moves to each blind, closing them, and finishing* L. ROBERT *moves to the upstage end of the desk*)

VICKIE (*rising*) I think I shall go to the pictures. Do they never give you any time off, Mr Goddard?

GODDARD. Actually, I'm off this evening.

VICKIE. How nice! (*Crossing below Goddard to* L *of him*) I think I shall go to the Odeon. The last programme starts at seven-fifteen. It's a smashing film.

GODDARD. What is it?

VICKIE. I don't know. Does it matter?

(VICKIE *exits up* C. GODDARD *follows into the doorway, watching her go. Then he re-enters to* R *of the doorway, leaving the door open.* MARIAN *crosses below the desk to the chair for her coat*)

MARIAN. Mr Westerby, I owe you an apology.

ROBERT. That's all right.

MARIAN. I was sure you were involved with her. (*She starts putting on her coat*)

ROBERT (*moving to* L *of her and helping her with her coat*) It was foolish of me to be concerned with other people's intrigues.

MARIAN. Perhaps they do love each other. What do you think?

ROBERT. I don't know.

MARIAN. This could bring them back together. That is—unless . . . At least he needed your help. (*She picks up her handbag*) There's nothing *I* can do. I've helped him all I can. I shan't be needed any more.

(MARIAN *exits up* C, *leaving the door open, then through the outer door, which she closes*)

ROBERT. What do you suppose she meant by that? "I've helped him all I can." (*Moving up* C) Well, now I'm playing the detective, and we've plenty of investigators, don't you agree?

GODDARD. Yes, sir. Mrs Piper and the Super make a formidable pair.

ROBERT. I'd better put those calls through. (*He moves down* R) Excuse me.

(ROBERT *exits down* R, *closing the door.* GODDARD *moves into the passage up* C, *standing* L *of the doorway.* MARSHALL *enters and comes into the room to up* R. BAXTER *follows, up* L *of the armchair.* GODDARD *exits up* C, *leaving the door open*)

MARSHAL (*as they enter*) So it suddenly struck me that if I could frighten Mrs Piper she'd panic . . .

BAXTER (*as they reach their positions*) So what do you suggest happened?

MARSHALL. Well, obviously somebody wants to get rid of me. Somebody who knew my wife was involved with Cameron. It's well known I'm jealous. If Cameron was found dead in these offices, who else would be suspected?

BAXTER. Suspicion wouldn't harm you, sir. There would have to be evidence against you.

MARSHALL. So he manufactured it. Don't you see, everything has been manufactured to trap me?

BAXTER (*moving above the desk for his hat and coat*) That's what they all say. I'm afraid you'll have to do better than that.

MARSHALL (*moving to the up R end of the desk*) If you don't believe me the trick has succeeded. It was planned in detail to have that effect. You don't believe me because I can't prove it. And he knew that would happen.

BAXTER. If it's going to be accepted, sir, it's got to be proved. (*He crosses Marshall to R of the desk, putting on his hat and coat*)

MARSHALL. I tell you I can't.

(MRS PIPER *enters up* C)

MRS PIPER. I can. (*She closes the door and moves to R of Baxter*)

BAXTER. Be quiet! (*He turns to face her*) What did you say?

MRS PIPER. I said I can prove that what he's saying is true.

BAXTER. If you have information hidden from me . . .

MRS PIPER. I've got nothing hidden from you. But I've got an idea.

BAXTER. Mrs Piper, because my heart is as soft as butter I have listened to as fanciful an explanation as I shall hear in a month of Sundays and now—*now* you have an idea. (*He crosses below her to the door up* C) Goddard!

MRS PIPER. Oo, he is stubborn! 'Arry (*to L of Baxter*) do you want to reproach yourself for the rest of your life?

BAXTER. No. That's why we're going to the police station. (*Moving down* RC) Goddard! Where's he got to?

MRS PIPER (*following to L of him*) You always was a hard man, 'Arry, but I always thought you was fair.

BAXTER. Well, just tell me one thing. If Mr Marshall didn't do it, who did?

MRS PIPER. Young Westerby.

BAXTER (*shouting*) Westerby!

MRS PIPER (*putting her hand over his mouth*) Ssshhh! (*She moves round to R of him*)

BAXTER. Why should he kill Cameron?

MRS PIPER. I don't know.

BAXTER. Why should he want to harm Mr Marshall?

MRS PIPER. I don't know that either.

BAXTER. Well, what do you know.

MRS PIPER. I know he done it. I don't know why but I know.

BAXTER. Oh! (*He turns away and moves up stage*)

MARSHALL (*moving to L of Baxter*) She says she's sure it's Westerby. That's why I say now's our only chance to prove it.

BAXTER. Has she any proof?

MARSHALL. Not exactly.

BAXTER (*angrily*) Well, I *have!* Against you!

MRS PIPER (*moving up to R of Baxter*) That's clever, that is, proving an innocent man committed a murder. 'Arry, I know a way to catch young Westerby out. But I'll need your help.

BAXTER. Ha! I'm not to be dismissed entirely!

MARSHALL. Give her a chance.

(BAXTER *considers. He has a profound inner struggle*)

BAXTER. I'll give you precisely ten minutes. (*Calling*) Goddard!

(BAXTER *moves up* C, *opens the door and stands* R *of it.* MRS PIPER *crosses up stage to Marshall.* GODDARD *comes in to* L *of Baxter*)

BAXTER. Where have you been?

GODDARD. Er—just checking on a few things, sir.

BAXTER. Come in and shut the door.

(GODDARD *does so*)

Ten minutes from now we leave this building. (*Moving* R) Mr Marshall will accompany us to the station.

GODDARD. Yes, sir.

(MRS PIPER *crosses below Goddard to* L *of Baxter*)

MRS PIPER. No. 'Arry, listen. I want this young feller to take Mr M. out, and I want *you* to stop here.

BAXTER. Why?

MRS PIPER. I'll tell you when we're alone. (*To Goddard*) Don't take him to the police station, it'll only be a waste of petrol. Pretend to go, come back and hang about outside. (*Turning to Baxter*) Let's have some action, 'Arry.

BAXTER (*shouting*) Go on, Goddard, you heard.

MRS PIPER. Oohh, 'Arry, you do shout!

GODDARD (*whispering*) Shall we wait outside for you, sir?

BAXTER (*whispering*) Come back in ten minutes.

(GODDARD *opens the door up* C. MARSHALL *crosses him to exit*)

GODDARD (*loudly*) Come along with me, sir. There's a car waiting downstairs. You'll have to come along to the station . . .

(GODDARD *and* MARSHALL *exit up* C. GODDARD *closes the door.* MRS PIPER *moves to* L *of Baxter, takes his hand and leads him below to down* LC)

MRS PIPER. Young Westerby—he's in there. In a tick I'm gonna

have him in here and then I shall ask him why he killed Mr Cameron
and Mr Logan.

BAXTER (R *of her*) That's a very good idea.

MRS PIPER. Yes.

BAXTER. There's only one snag. He won't tell you.

MRS PIPER. You'll be surprised. He'll tell me all right.

BAXTER. Carry on! I'll watch. (*He sits in the chair* R *of the desk*)

(MRS PIPER *pulls him up*)

MRS PIPER. Oh, you can't sit there. He wouldn't say a word if
he knew you were listening.

BAXTER. Ah, you want me to wait outside. (*He moves up* C)

MRS PIPER. No. Inside. (*She follows him, pulling his coat*)

BAXTER. Inside what?

MRS PIPER. This cupboard. (*She opens the door of the cupboard,
standing* L *of it*)

BAXTER (*loudly*) Do you expect me to get in there?

MRS PIPER. Ssh! (*She puts her hand over his mouth and moves round to*
R *of him*) There's nowhere else, is there?

BAXTER. I can think of *several* alternatives.

MRS PIPER. You promised to help.

BAXTER. I did not undertake to squeeze into a cupboard.

MRS PIPER. There won't be any squeezing, darling. You're
quite slim. Specially in that coat.

(MRS PIPER *struggles with* BAXTER *who protests, but finally she pushes
him into the cupboard and closes the door with his arm still sticking out.*
BAXTER *withdraws his arm and* MRS PIPER *closes the door. Loud bangs
and shouts from inside the cupboard*)

MRS PIPER. Don't make no noise, 'Arry.

(*The knocking continues and* MRS PIPER *moves to sit in the chair* R
of the desk. She picks up the ashtray and knocks the desk leg with it.
ROBERT *enters down* R. *The knocking from* BAXTER *stops*)

ROBERT. What's going on in here? There's a lot of noise.

(MRS PIPER *turns*)

MRS PIPER. I didn't hear no noise, dear. This desk leg's collo-
lopsed. (*She continues knocking with the ashtray*)

(ROBERT *turns to go.* MRS PIPER *puts the ashtray on the desk*)

Oh, Mr Westerby . . .

(ROBERT *stops.* MRS PIPER *rises, above the armchair*)

ROBERT. Yes.

MRS PIPER. Did you hear they've arrested Mr Marshall, dear?

ROBERT. Well, it was inevitable, wasn't it? (*He turns to go*)

MRS PIPER. Mr Westerby! Could you spare me a minute of your
time?

ROBERT. I'm very busy, Mrs Piper. What is it?

MRS PIPER (R *of the armchair*) Well, when this murder took place the last person I'd have suspected was you.

ROBERT. I should hope so.

MRS PIPER. But then one or two things happened that made me wonder.

ROBERT (*moving a pace towards her*) Wonder what?

MRS PIPER. If I hadn't been wrong. You see, Mr Westerby, liking you as I do I don't want to tell the police what I know.

ROBERT. Tell them what, Mrs Piper?

MRS PIPER. That it wasn't Mr Marshall Mr Cameron asked for that night—it was you.

ROBERT. Me? It couldn't have been.

MRS PIPER. Another thing, Mr Westerby, you said you'd never seen Mr Cameron.

ROBERT. Certainly.

MRS PIPER. But when I said he had a scar across his face you looked surprised.

ROBERT. Did I? (*He crosses below her to* LC, *facing up stage*) I don't remember.

MRS PIPER. I do. (*Moving above the armchair*) If you'd never seen him you wouldn't be surprised whether he had a scar or not. 'Cos he hadn't got a scar, had he? And another thing, Mr Westerby—you told the Superintendent you didn't know Mr Logan was back in London.

ROBERT. Yes.

MRS PIPER. Well, that wasn't true, was it? You see, when I was at his flat I told Mr Logan about this bother we was having and do you know what he said? He said: "I'll give Westerby a ring and have a word with him."

ROBERT. Did he?

MRS PIPER. Well, if he rung you, you must have known he was here.

ROBERT. Did you hear him ring me?

MRS PIPER. I heard him say he was going to.

ROBERT (*taking a step towards the fire-escape*) Perhaps he changed his mind.

MRS PIPER (*sitting on the* L *arm of the armchair*) Then that's all right then. Because Baxter can check with the phone people and they'll confirm that Mr Logan didn't call you.

ROBERT. You can't check calls, Mrs Piper. Not with the automatic exchange.

MRS PIPER. It isn't automatic—not at Surbiton—you speak to the operator.

ROBERT. So you do.

MRS PIPER. Well, thank you, Mr Westerby. (*She rises to above the chair* R *of the desk*) I'm glad we cleared that up.

ROBERT (*moving to* C) Are you going to tell all this to the police?

MRS PIPER. I've got no choice, have I?

ROBERT. No, Mrs Piper, you haven't. (*He crosses below her to the door up* C, *locks it and pockets the key*)

MRS PIPER. Mr Westerby, you've locked that door.

ROBERT. So I have. (*He moves down* R, *locks the door, and pockets the key*)

(MRS PIPER *follows to up* R *of the armchair*)

MRS PIPER. Mr Westerby, you've murdered two men.

ROBERT. Yes, Mrs Piper, I have.

MRS PIPER. Well, that's not very nice, is it, dear? What did you want to do it for? You must have had a very good reason.

ROBERT. Oh, yes! I had a very good reason. I don't mind telling you about it under the circumstances. It will be nice to have—(*taking her round the armchair to below it*) someone to confide in. I think you'd better sit down, Mrs Piper.

MRS PIPER (*attempting to rise*) No, I'd just as soon stand.

ROBERT (*pushing her down*) Sit down, Mrs Piper. Yes, in one stroke I got rid of the two men I hate most, Cameron and Marshall. (*He moves below to* L *of the armchair*) You see, I want Claire. And with Cameron dead I'd have no opposition. She likes me. She likes me a great deal. And, with Marshall out of the way I'll take over the business as well. (*He moves slowly down* L) It really was ingenious, you know. I sent Cameron a letter signed "Marshall", asking him to meet me here at eight-fifteen. When he turned up I was waiting for him. Meanwhile, Marshall was in the café waiting for the non-existent Mr Warfield. Do you understand?

MRS PIPER. I don't see why you had to harm poor Mr Logan.

ROBERT. Ah! Well, now—for the last couple of years or so Mr Logan and I have been dipping our hands into the till. We were both pretty smart lads, as you yourself often remarked, Mrs Piper. (*He moves slowly to* L *of the armchair*) He also knew how I felt about Claire. So, when you called on him and told him what was going on here, do you know he suspected me? Me, Mrs Piper. Yes, he did phone me. He said he didn't mind being a thief, but he drew the line at murder. He was going to tell the police. Well, now, I couldn't have that, could I? (*He moves round* L *of the armchair to above it, taking off his tie*) I had to get rid of him—I'm very sorry, Mrs Piper—I'm terribly fond of you—but now I shall have to get rid of you. (*He leans over her, trying to loop the tie round her neck*)

MRS PIPER (*rising, to* L *of the armchair*) I got news for you, Mr Westerby. Superintendent Baxter's in that cupboard. He's heard every word you've said.

ROBERT. You're bluffing, Mrs Piper.

MRS PIPER. All right, then, you watch. We'll see if I'm bluffing. (*She moves up to* L *of the cupboard and takes the handle in her* R *hand*) You can come out now, 'Arry. (*She pulls, and the handle comes away in her hand. She screams, puts the handle in the ashtray on the desk, and attempts to move to the fire exit below the desk)*

(ROBERT *intercepts her.* MRS PIPER *moves away up* C. ROBERT *pulls the desk towards him and moves up stage,* R *of it.* MRS PIPER *runs* R, *picks up the small chair and throws it at him. He pushes it aside down stage.* MRS PIPER *turns out the lights up* C, *and in the black-out moves to the up* C *window and hides behind the curtain.* ROBERT *turns the lights on, circles down stage to* LC, *turns and sees Mrs Piper and, moving up to* L *of her, rips the curtain down. As it envelops him,* MRS PIPER *escapes to the light switch up* C)

MRS PIPER. 'Arry! Tell him you're in there! (*She switches out the lights and hides under the table* R)

(ROBERT *moves up* C *and turns the lights on. He moves down to Mrs Piper and tries to pull her out. She turns the waste-paper basket over his head and escapes, running down* R *and turning the lights out again from the switch there. In the black-out she hides behind the plant up* R, *taking out the concealed leaf.* ROBERT *pulls the basket from his head, turns on the lights from down* R, *sees Mrs Piper and moves up to* L *of her. He throws the plant over.* MRS PIPER *is revealed holding the leaf over her eyes.* ROBERT *grabs her and pulls her towards the armchair)*

(*As they struggle to the armchair*) No, Mr Westerby, I capifilate. Think of your mum.

(GODDARD *and* MARSHALL *enter up* C. *They seize Robert, who falls to the floor up* R *of the armchair.* MARSHALL *pulls him up,* R *of him*)

GODDARD. What's going on here?
MRS PIPER. Oh, my gawd! I never been chased like it.
GODDARD (L *of Robert*) Are you all right, Mrs Piper?
MRS PIPER. Just.

(BAXTER *knocks from the cupboard*)

GODDARD. Ssh! What's that?
MRS PIPER. It's 'Arry having kittens in the cupboard.
GODDARD (*moving to the cupboard door*) There's no handle.
MRS PIPER. It's on the desk, dear.

(GODDARD *takes the handle and puts it in the door.* MRS PIPER *moves to the desk, picks up the file and stands* L *of the cupboard.* GODDARD *opens the door and helps to pull Baxter out.* BAXTER *collapses on the floor.* MRS PIPER *fans him with the file*)

Slap his face, dear.

(GODDARD *does so*)

Harder, dear. Let him feel it.

(GODDARD *does so.* BAXTER *jumps up.* GODDARD *rises*)

BAXTER. Goddard, what the hell do you think you're doing?

(MRS PIPER *replaces the file on the desk*)

GODDARD. I'm sorry, sir. What were you doing in there?
BAXTER. Waiting for a twenty-eight bus. (*To Mrs Piper*) Why didn't you let me out?

(GODDARD *moves back to take over guarding Robert, and* MARSHALL *moves up stage*)

MRS PIPER. The handle came away in my hand.
BAXTER. It would!
MRS PIPER. 'Arry, my life was in danger. What a time to take a nap!
BAXTER. Take a nap? I nearly died in your blasted cupboard.

(MRS PIPER *sits in the chair* R *of the desk.* MARSHALL *moves slowly round picking up the plant and closing the cupboard door*)

(*To Robert*) Robert Westerby, I'm arresting you for the murder of James Cameron, and it's my duty to warn you that anything you say may be taken down and used in evidence.
ROBERT. Save your breath! If I'm not smart enough to outwit her I give up.
BAXTER. Are you willing to make a statement?
ROBERT. If it'll please you. (*To Mrs Piper*) You old bitch!
MRS PIPER. Oo, Harry—did you hear what he called you?

(BAXTER, GODDARD *and* ROBERT *talk together quietly down* R. ROBERT *signs the confession at the table*)

MARSHALL (*to Mrs Piper, moving above the desk*) I don't know how to thank you.
MRS PIPER. You could make me a director.
MARSHALL. I will.
MRS PIPER. No—I'll be satisfied with a golden handshake.
BAXTER (*to Goddard*) Take him to the car. I'll follow.

(GODDARD *takes Robert up to the door*)

ROBERT (*at the door*) I do apologize, Mrs Piper. I shouldn't have tried to strangle you.
MRS PIPER. It's quite all right, dear.
ROBERT. I should have broken your bloody neck.

(GODDARD *takes* ROBERT *off up* C)

MRS PIPER (*rising and moving down* R) I don't want to play with him no more. He's too rough. (*She starts to tidy up the papers on the desk and the floor, putting them in the waste-paper basket*)
BAXTER (*moving up to Marshall*) Hadn't you better run along and tell your wife, sir?
MARSHALL. Am I free to go?

Mrs Piper. Yes, dear, we shan't be needing you no more.

(Marshall *moves to the door*)

Baxter. Just one thing, Mr Marshall. The button. I suppose you took it?

Marshall. Oh, yes.

Baxter. You'd better let me have it.

(Marshall *gives him the button*)

Mrs Piper (*looking up from her tidying*) Was it you who . . . ?

Marshall. I'm sorry.

Mrs Piper. You cheeky thing!

(Marshall *hesitates, then kisses her and exits up* c)

He kissed me! I've never been kissed by a tycoon. Did you hear, 'Arry? He's going to make me his sleeping partner! (*She continues tidying*)

Baxter. Well, I hope you're satisfied, Lily.

Mrs Piper (*continuing to tidy the papers*) I hope you are. I cleared that little lot up for you pretty smart, didn't I?

Baxter (*above the armchair*) I'd have cleared it up for myself if you hadn't withheld evidence. You should have told me Logan said he was going to ring Westerby.

Mrs Piper. He didn't. (*She puts the basket down* r)

Baxter. But you told Westerby . . . ˙

Mrs Piper (r *of Baxter*) I was only guessing.

Baxter (*shaking his finger at her*) He didn't say he'd ring him, did he?

Mrs Piper. 'Course he didn't. (*She bites his finger and crosses below him to pick up the chair and replace it up* r)

Baxter. Very clever. (*Moving up to face her*) Well, I've got news for you, Mrs Knowall. We couldn't have traced Logan's call to Westerby—not even from Surbiton.

Mrs Piper. Fancy you knowing that, 'Arry Baxter. (*Moving to him*) I took a Gallup poll about it in the pub. Asked nine people. There was one yes, one no, four don't-knows, and the rest was sloshed. So I was pretty sure Mr Westerby wouldn't know neither.

Baxter. You crafty old . . .

Mrs Piper (*putting her hand over his mouth*) 'Arry! (*She takes her hand down*) You know, you weren't half a sport, getting in that cupboard. You did look daft when we opened the door. (*Crossing below him to the downstage end of the desk*) 'Ere, give us a hand with the desk, darling.

Baxter. All right, love. (*He moves to the upstage end of the desk*) Where does it go?

(*They move the desk to its correct position*)

This all right for you?

MRS PIPER. Yes, dear. (*She moves below the desk to* R *of it, tidying it*)
BAXTER (*moving to* C) Lily, I'm sorry if sometimes I lost my sense
of humour.
MRS PIPER. Which sense of humour?

(*They both laugh.* BAXTER *goes to the table down* R *for the confession*)

BAXTER. We mustn't keep Mr Westerby waiting. (*His jollity
evaporates*) My God, it's gone!
MRS PIPER. What's gone this time?
BAXTER (*moving to the armchair*) The signed confession.
MRS PIPER. Where's it gone to?
BAXTER. How the hell do I know?
MRS PIPER (*crossing below him to the table down* R) It was on there.
BAXTER. I know it was on there.
MRS PIPER. Harry, you are careless!
BAXTER (*stamping to* C; *roaring*) Everything disappears. Every-
thing bloody well vanishes!
MRS PIPER. You're raising your voice again. (*She is about to place
the basket under the table*)
BAXTER. Wait a minute! (*He glares at her*) Give me that basket!
(*He grabs the basket from her and upturns it on the floor* C)

They kneel side by side, facing the audience, going over the pile of papers
from the basket. From them he holds up the confession. He shakes his head
sadly and "threatens" her with the back of his hand, as—

the CURTAIN *falls*

FURNITURE AND PROPERTY LIST

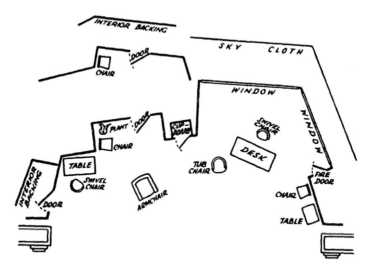

ACT I

Scene 1

On stage: Typist's table (down R) *On it:* paper file, typing paper, pen, pencil, shorthand pad, ashtray, typewriter with cover on, calender, telephone. *Under it:* waste-paper basket

Swivel chair (down R)

Upright chair (up R)

Armchair (LC)

Desk (up LC) *On it:* 2 telephones, 2 ashtrays, notepad, pencil, phone pad, large leather blotter (closed), pen tray with pens and pencils, photo, spectacles (MARSHALL), lighter, Anglepoise lamp

Swivel chair (above desk)

Tub chair (down R of desk). *On it:* blood

Table (down L) *On it:* lamp, ashtray, lighter

Upright chair (down L)

Rubber plant in pot (up R)

On windows: Venetian blinds fixed down permanently, curtains, upstage one able to be drawn up and put on press studs R end above runners for Act III

On wainscoting under table R: practical plug for Hoover
In cupboard: coats, hangers
On floor: carpet, rug under desk
On walls: pictures, picture calendars·
On outer door: thread and screw eye for slam effect
Door down R, closed
Door up C, open
Outer blind, open
Blinds shut
Curtains, open

SCENE 2

Personal: GODDARD: pen, notepad
        BAXTER: handkerchief
              watch
              pen, notepad
        MRS PIPER: bunch of keys

SCENE 3

Strike: Bloodstained chair

Check: Blinds open
      All doors closed

Set: Knife on desk
    Armchair to original position

Off stage: Empty waste-paper basket (MRS PIPER)

Personal: CLAIRE: handbag. *In it:* handkerchief
        ROBERT: filled cigarette-case
              lighter
        MARIAN: handbag. *In it:* key
        VICKIE: handbag

ACT II

Strike: Knife from desk
      Handbag from desk
      Blood from chair off up C

Check: Door up c half open with key off-stage side
Door down R closed
Outer door closed

Set: Hoover plugged in
Bucket with brush, 2 dusters, rags, down R
Carrier bag with bottle and rags on chair up R
Evening Standard in armchair (for MRS PIPER)
Desk blotter open
Open jotting pad on desk
Open spectacles L of blotter
Shorthand pad and pencil on table R
Empty tin below cupboard

Off stage: Briefcase containing papers and letters (MARSHALL)
File (ROBERT)
Briefcase (ROBERT)
Umbrella (VICKIE)
Tub chair (GODDARD)
Mallet for knocking (GODDARD)
Tray. *On it:* 5 cups, 5 saucers, spoons, tea, milk, sugar (GODDARD)

Personal: MRS PIPER: spectacles
keys with initials
button
BAXTER: handkerchief
CLAIRE: handbag
MARSHALL: note
VICKIE: watch

ACT III

Strike: Tea tray
Cleaning materials

Set: Full waste-paper basket under table R
Keys on stage side of both doors
Spare key off up c
MARIAN's coat in cupboard
MARIAN's handbag on table R
File with papers on table R
Plant slightly down stage
Spare leaf in plant

Check: Curtain on press studs to fall
Blinds open

L curtain open
Door down R closed
Outer door closed
Door up C open
Typewriter still uncovered
Blotter on desk closed
Cupboard door handle to pull off

Off stage: Cup of tea and spoon (VICKIE)
File of papers (ROBERT)
Brandy flask with one cap-full of brandy (MRS PIPER)
Spare key (GODDARD)

Personal: CLAIRE: handbag. *In it:* filled cigarette-case
ROBERT: lighter
MARSHALL: button

LIGHTING PLOT

Property fittings required: chandelier, Anglepoise lamp (not practical), table lamp, wall lamp above table R, wall brackets in hall

Interior. An office. The same scene throughout

THE APPARENT SOURCE OF LIGHT is a large window up L

THE MAIN ACTING AREAS are down R, RC, up RC, up C, C, up LC and LC

ACT I, SCENE 1. Night

To open: Wall lamp above table R only on. L half of room in darkness

Cue 1   MRS PIPER switches lights on from up C   (Page 1)
Snap on all interior lights

Cue 2   At close of scene   (Page 1)
Quick fade to Black-Out

ACT I, SCENE 2. Night

To open: All interior lights on

Cue 3   BAXTER turns on light in room off down R   (Page 7)
Snap on strip off R

ACT I, SCENE 3. Morning

To open: Effect of morning light. All brackets, lamps, chandelier off

No cues

ACT II. Evening

To open: All interior lights and strip off down R on

Cue 4   MARSHALL (unseen) switches off lights from up C   (Page 39)
Snap to Black-Out

Cue 5   GODDARD switches on lights from down R   (Page 39)
Snap up to opening lighting

ACT III. Afternoon

To open: Effect of dull daylight outside. All interior lights on

Cue 6   MRS PIPER: "It doesn't satisfy me."   (Page 60)
Start slow fade outside to dusk

Cue 7   MARIAN closes blinds   (Page 65)
Complete previous cue

Cue 8   MRS PIPER switches off lights from up C   (Page 71)
Snap out all interior lighting

Cue 9	ROBERT switches lights from up c *Reverse Cue 8*	(Page 71)
Cue 10	MRS PIPER switches off lights from up c *Snap out all interior lighting*	(Page 71)
Cue 11	ROBERT switches lights on from up c *Reverse Cue 10*	(Page 71)

EFFECTS PLOT

ACT I

SCENE 1

Cue 1   MRS PIPER dials a number   (Page 1)
         Outer door slams

SCENE 2

Cue 2   MRS PIPER: ". . . to make me see double."   (Page 4)
         Outer door slams

SCENE 3

No cues

ACT II

Cue 3   MRS PIPER: ". . . lost in a fog."   (Page 40)
         Outer door slams

Cue 4   CLAIRE: "I do."   (Page 47)
         Telephone on desk rings

ACT III

No cues

CPSIA information can be obtained at www.ICGtesting.com
Printed in the USA
LVOW101533270612

287927LV00010B/143/P